THIRSTY **HEART**

NOURISHMENT FOR A DEHYDRATED SOUL

REGINA FOREST

Publisher: Planted Press
ISBN-13: 978-0997949803 (Planted Press)
ISBN-10: 0997949805

Cover Design: Trent Meistrell and Jason Darrah
Interior design and layout: Fusion Creative Works, fusioncw.com

Follow at:
Thirstyheartbook.com
Facebook: Thirsty Heart, Regina Forest
Instagram: @thirstyheartbook, @reg4est
Twitter: @ReginaForest
Blog: reg4est.wordpress.com
Bridgerelationships.com

TO THE LOVES OF MY LIFE…

JESUS
my very heartbeat

JOHN
my one and only

JOSHUA
HAYLIE
CHARLES
FAITH
MADDISON
PARKER
SILAS
my delight and treasure

In memory of

Haylie Anne Forest
My Hero of Grace

8.11.84 – 9.30.86

Her life and death have etched true beauty on my heart,
soul, life, family, and future—more than mere
words could ever express.

*Love you forever my sweet daughter—
until we meet again...*

CONTENTS

FOREWORD

When you wake up in the morning, you are considered alive. Your eyes are open. Your heart is beating, you're breathing, and the rest of your body is functioning. But would you consider yourself living? Besides the fact that your body is working, are your heart, soul, and spirit alive and well? Could you attest to the fact that in the depths of your being, you are satisfied and content?

I know there have been seasons where I would say I wasn't truly living and I was dead inside, but no one would have ever guessed or noticed. I would open my eyes on a clear, sunny day, yet for me, it was hazy.

Life has a way of bringing pain and suffering, and though it would be nice to blame someone or something, it does not actually fix the problem. People who live free and unrestricted are those who live in God's grace, those who choose to seek answers for their situations and cut through the fluff to be truly transformed. *Thirsty Heart* is a guidebook for just that—no more guessing, no more wasted hours, no more hopeless days.

As the author's daughter, I can testify to the quenched thirst in my mom's life. I remember as a child thinking to myself, *Why does she cry so much? Life really isn't that bad.* Little did I know the deep heartache she suffered.

There were years piled on years of my mom continually going to God and laying down her entire life in surrender. She would pour her heart out, struggle to be satisfied, and in the end, she always found Jesus to be enough. This attitude of surrender to God has never left her dry. After years of tears, something shifted.

When I was twenty-two years old, my mom and dad opened up to our family with the truth regarding their marriage. They were able to share about how their encounter with God's unconditional love and grace helped them pioneer through the process of healing and forgiveness. This is when the revelation of God's goodness and power really sank in. My siblings and I could all see that lives surrendered to God can truly be transformed.

The drastic difference in my parents' lives is unexplainable and, to be honest, unbelievable. There is no way, apart from Jesus, someone with their past and experiences should be walking in freedom and wholeness. How can two people with a history like theirs possibly find a reason to wake up, take a deep breath, and love their lives? Well, obviously by their transformation, they encountered something very real and miraculous.

I believe in the power of God in my mom's story. I believe that the same power in her life can absolutely encounter your life.

If you find yourself in need of something real and sustainable, look no further. Welcome to wisdom. Drink deep the insight of *Thirsty Heart* and find the satisfaction you have always desired.

Maddison Meistrell
Daughter of the Author
Youth Pastor, City Bible Church
Portland, Oregon

For I will pour water on him who is thirsty,
And floods on the dry ground.

–Isaiah 44:3a

INTRODUCTION

Thirsty Heart was birthed during a very dark period of my life. It was a time of deep suffering and sorrow where my heart and life were shattered. If suffering had a limit, then my capacity had long since reached its quota. I guess you could say writing *Thirsty Heart* was the therapy Jesus used to get me through this devastating time in my life. He has brought enormous healing and growth to my life through this book, as I pray He will do for you as you read it.

As a child, father issues and sexual abuse opened the doors for rejection, abandonment, and fear to grip my life. As a teenager, I used alcohol and the attention I received from boys to mask my emptiness. During those years, I also had two abortions, which led to further brokenness.

I married an equally broken person. Both of us were just beginning our journey with Christ, struggling to get our lives together, which I suppose caused the devil to keep busy harassing us. At one point in our marriage, we had seven out of the top ten problems that cause couples to divorce. Death seemed to invade our lives with three miscarriages and the untimely deaths of our second child and my only brother. Marital unfaithfulness and financial issues were ever present in our lives. I also experienced the heartbreak of a broken relationship with my family. With all these issues, I lived in a constant tension of fear and dread. I dreaded my future, living in fear that it would resemble my past, making it difficult to live in the present.

Every time a trial came my way, I was upset with God and a thankful word could not be found on my lips or in my heart. I had a false mind-set that I had experienced enough pain for a lifetime—not realizing there is no meter on suffering. I wrongly figured when I reached my quota of suffering, it simply would cease. Then I could get on with my life, free of further heartache.

You can imagine the huge disappointment that accompanied my sorrow when I found myself yet again in the school of suffering.

A friend and leader in our church, whom we have since forgiven, betrayed us. It turned out he was a Ponzi scheme artist. After he and his wife built a relationship of trust with my husband and me, they conned us and we, along with many others, lost our home. We lost our investment property and the home our kids grew up in. While they were at fault, I blamed my husband and myself more. Although we had been on our journey with Christ for over a quarter of a century, we did not have the relationship with Jesus we should have had. We mainly lived for ourselves, so we listened to the voice of greed that always accompanies a self-indulgent lifestyle, instead of listening to the voice of wisdom.

This financial tragedy happened simultaneously with the recession. Not only did we lose our home, but our business, which was grossing over a hundred thousand dollars a year, plummeted to earning zero dollars. It was a season where almost everything was a disaster.

Facing betrayal, the upheaval of finances, and losing our home was devastating, but the main anguish came from unfaithfulness in our marriage. I thought my husband had long since dealt with his adultery issues, but I learned after twenty-five years it was still very much a part of our marriage relationship.

I believe what was so painful was that God did not agree with my desire to divorce my husband. He wanted me to change my heart, not my marital status. After so many years, I was done—my love and patience had reached their end. Thankfully, Jesus' mercy for the both of us had not run dry. I had to face the biggest decision of my life. My choices were to either humble and submit myself to God's will for my heart and marriage, or do my own will. To "Me" the first choice resembled stepping into a fiery furnace and the latter freedom. I am so grateful that the grace of God led me to choose submission.

In a way, choosing God's will walked me through a fiery furnace, but after years of selfish living, I needed refining. Jesus asked me to make Him enough and to be a bridge to my husband. I needed to put my heart and life in His hands—to let Him meet my every need and lay down my rights and life. And in doing so, my husband could experience grace in the form of forgiving, unrestricted love, which would assist him in finding Jesus' love. I was to love my husband as Jesus loves me, with tender mercy that suffers long and heals compassionately by its unconditional love, and to be an instrument to help heal his brokenness, leading his heart to what really matters—salvation. My position in being a bridge to my husband meant just that—laying down my life as a path for him to walk on, with no guarantees he would even choose to take the bridge that led to Jesus.

This, no doubt, was a tall order!

The work that had to be done in my heart and soul was immense. I needed to trust Jesus and let Him heal my broken life first. My old ways of protecting my heart by putting up walls could no longer be my default method for handling life. My former ways of disdaining my husband, treating him as my enemy, and expecting him to fail in life had to come to an end. Jesus was calling me to surrender and submit my entire heart, will, mind, emotions, marriage, and life to Him alone. I had to learn to make Him enough for my entire life.

I am no goody two-shoes—that's for sure. I even prayed for my husband's death so I could just be free of him and his sin—free from the pain of heartbreak. But merciful Jesus wanted the best for my husband and for me. My husband went to church but did not know Jesus personally and had yet to give Him his heart. I truly believe if he would have died in his sin, he would have gone to hell. Once I realized this, I had to examine who I was as a person—who I was at the core of my being.

I realized that loving my husband through his sin and brokenness was what I should have been doing all along. If I could not forgive and unconditionally love *my own husband* (the man I vowed before God to love and the only person I am one with), then whom could I love? If I could not love him through his weakness, what would that say about me as a person?

I also understood it was the devil I was really fighting against (not my husband). The enemy of my soul, the one who comes to kill, steal, and destroy, did not want my marriage to succeed. And I did not want him to devastate and level my family through divorce. No, I would not give him the satisfaction nor put my family through that. Besides, if the work of the cross is enough, why would I not let Jesus do His work in my heart, life, and marriage?

As I surrendered to God's will, He healed me and made all the fragmented pieces of my heart whole. And in turn, I was able to love my husband and be the bridge for him to find Jesus and become whole.

It was brutal but only because I had to die to my selfishness and say good-bye to my old friend—fear. The outcome of pressing through was worth the agony.

The season of surrender and learning to be filled with Jesus brought healing to all issues both past and present. I have definitely learned through this process to see people as God sees them, to look at their hearts instead of their behavior. I have come to the understanding that I cannot change anyone, but I can love them and let God change them.

My faith in God has been strengthened, helping me to stop treating Him like a genie in a bottle, and it took me from only knowing about Jesus to an actual relationship where I now know and trust Him. My dehydrated heart drank from the Living Water and came alive through Jesus' unfathomable, faithful love. He drew me to the place where I now live my life, close to His heart, covered by His love and grace, with an understanding of my need for Him. I am no longer defined by my suffering, heartache, or sin. I have a clearer knowledge of who I am in Christ, realizing I am not identified by what I can do for Jesus but by what He has done for me.

This is not to say I have arrived. I am in process, as we all are. I understand that life goes on and trials of various kinds are guaranteed. Pain and sorrow will come and go. The difference is I now live life from the stance of thankfulness, counting trials as joy. Suffering has led me to the deepest of thirsts that only Jesus has been able to quench. Since my faith is stronger, I am no longer an unbelieving believer. I have emerged fully convinced of God's faithfulness.

As I daily seek Jesus, my heart is hydrated and full. Circumstances do not dictate my life. I am no longer under the thumb of oppression, and the best news is neither is my husband!

My hope, prayer, and expectation are that this book will be a bridge to every dehydrated heart, soul, and life it comes in contact with, making a way for people to quench their thirsty hearts. It has been designed to help people take steps in heart hydration, no matter the cause of the dehydration. As you read this, please focus on Jesus' faithfulness. Also, please stretch your faith to believe that you personally—your heart and life—will be healed, restored, and hydrated.

1

HEART HYDRATION

Signs of dehydration can catch you off guard. I remember when one of my teenage daughters was taking a few dance classes and decided she also wanted to play ice hockey—quite the contrast, I know. She became the ballerina goalie!

Almost every evening my daughter would go to dance class, hockey practice, or a game, and almost every day we would find her lying on the couch with flu-like symptoms. After a couple of weeks, we decided to take her to the doctor. Upon hearing the symptoms, the doctor's conclusion was simple: my daughter was suffering from dehydration.

This is often how heart dehydration sneaks up on us. Sometimes we are walking down life's road unaware of how thirsty our hearts really are. Other times, we may have an understanding that something is just not right, but we are unable to pinpoint the issue.

As with my daughter, my dehydration sneaked up on me, except that I was not only spent physically—my heart and soul were also heavy, broken, and parched from life. I certainly was not living the abundant life Jesus came to give me (John 10:10b).

The telltale signs of my dehydration were as plain as day. In my own way, I was lying on the couch of life, feeling achy and tired, lethargically going through the motions of my life but not really living.

I called myself a believer but was filled with doubt. I was happy but lacked joy, busy but empty and bored, surrounded by people but lonely. I smiled, but inside I was rude, cynical, skeptical, and suspicious. I was safe, but fear held me. I had given my life to Jesus, but I could not really let it go. I called Him Lord but never let Him *be* Lord. I knew *about* God but did not know Him personally. I walked up to the fountain of life but only sipped; therefore, my heart, life, and soul were dehydrated.

These are common issues. We know Jesus can be enough to fill the dry longing, but we strive for other lovers. We fill in our gaps with everything but what really satisfies. And sadly, we don't live the life Jesus intends for us to live, a life lived in the fullness of His love and grace.

If there is lack or dehydration in your heart, soul, or life, then one or more of the following issues may be the cause:

- lack an intimate relationship with Jesus
- struggle with your identity in Christ
- never feel good enough for God
- struggle to understand God's grace
- hold a grudge against God
- live outside the provision of the cross
- struggle with selfishness
- have trouble with submission
- struggle to make Jesus enough
- have weak faith, trust, or belief
- struggle to be thankful
- struggle with love and obedience
- are brokenhearted
- struggle with forgiveness
- suffer from sexual brokenness
- feel damaged from the messiness of life

Because of our craving humanity, we are always searching for the answers to what will bring happiness or what will make our lives worth living—something to fill our lack. In order to move past a life of continual searching, we must first recognize the answer is not a tool of some sort but a relationship. A personal, thriving relationship with Jesus Christ is the cure to heart dehydration. If you already have a relationship with Jesus and your heart still shows signs of dehydration, I encourage you to go deeper and dare to know Him more. Jesus tells us, "To all who are thirsty I will give freely from the springs of the water of life" (Revelations 21:6b, NLT). Jesus *is* the "springs of the water of life," and therefore the only answer to our hearts' dry longing. A relationship with Jesus is our anchor and base for all we are and do. Essentially, our lives must stem from Him.

Please understand me clearly. I did not say going to church or doing "Christian stuff" is the answer. I love church and I believe in the importance of the local church. Every believer should attend and be an active part of the body of Christ. The reason I am specifying this is because a lot of people think sitting in church is the answer to the longing of their heart and to gaining salvation. My former Pastor, Steve Meistrell, would quite often say: "You can sit in McDonald's all day long, and you will never turn into a hamburger." This is true about church too; we can sit in church all our lives and never be a believer or follower of Christ. Consequently, we will not come into a relationship with Jesus and our thirsty hearts may never be quenched. And so, an authentic, two-way relationship with Jesus is the answer to heart dehydration.

Sounds simple enough, but most people want a tool, an impersonal tool, something to just fill in the gap. Why? A tool does not require an investment of our hearts, souls, time, energy, and lives, but a relationship does.

That was my story, and I owned every single one of the issues I listed earlier. My heart and life were wanting and dry, and even after becoming a believer and follower of Christ, I was still searching. The list to why I did not settle in and devote my life to a relationship with Jesus was pretty long. I believe my fundamental issues were unbelief, fear, and self. I was just looking for something to add to my life, a tool—an instrument to make me happy. It is true Jesus is an instrument to happiness, but the struggle happens when that is all we let Him be. I can attest that our hearts will continue to thirst until He becomes our very life. The sooner we figure this out, the better off we are.

Reexamine the list of issues. If you can say yes to one of these areas being even a slight problem, then you are on the right track to heart hydration.

THE BOTTOM LINE

The foundation to heart hydration is no huge mystery, and after you read my answer, you may roll your eyes and think you have heard it all before. I am stating the obvious, only because it will not be mentioned very much throughout the book. I just want you to have a clear understanding of the basis for all you will read. Okay, so now I will tell you. The bottom line is love. (Did you roll your eyes?) I know the "L" word gets tossed around quite a bit. But God's love really is the bottom line to any kind of spiritual progression.

Since a relationship with Jesus is how we are to hydrate our thirsty hearts, souls, and lives, then we primarily have to accept and know God the Father's love, which He demonstrated in such a great act of love by sending Jesus to redeem us. First John 4:9–10 tells us of this perfect love: "God showed how much he loved us by sending his one and only Son into the world so that we might have eternal life through him. This is real love—not that we loved God, but that he loved us and sent his Son as a sacrifice to take away our sins" (NLT).

Jesus was sent not only to redeem us, but this love, this Jesus, made a path for relationship. He loves us and wants to be with us. We were made for this relationship. When the relationship piece is out of alignment, our hearts will be found dry—dehydrated. Jesus, in His willingness to obey the Father's will, removed the veil that stood between us and God, and with this action, He made a path for relationship. Prior to the cross, man could not relate with God the way we now do, which is why priests, sacrifices, and rituals were needed. The people brought their sacrifice to the priests, and the priests went into the holy place and made an offering for them.

Thankfully, it has changed. Jesus was the final sacrifice, and now we are honored to live in a personal relationship with Him. This brings us back to the bottom line of love; our relationship with Jesus is based in love, and if this part is not in place, we will always lack. Think about it. What happens to marriage relationships where love is absent or has grown cold? They are just that—cold and business-like with little or no intimacy or communication.

I have been married for thirty-four years, and we absolutely have had our loveless times where intimacy and communication were void. I understand the effort required in marriage and what it looks like to be a good spouse. And undoubtedly, love is always the primary component. Why do two people give up their lives, become one, submit, and serve each other anyway?

The answer is love.

It is the same in our relationship with Christ. We cannot love, have faith in, and submit to Him unless we trust, know, receive, and live in His love. Perfect love is what He has for us. All we need to do is receive and own it.

PERFECT LOVE

A most amazing aspect of this perfect love is that Jesus loves us unconditionally. I know the term "unconditional love" is often overused, but actually, it has a rather wonderful meaning. Let your heart drink in the truth that there are no conditions to God's love for you. There is nothing in your past that would cause Him to stop loving you, and there is nothing in your future that will make Him love you more or less. Ponder that for a moment. You are loved no matter what—no performances needed. He loves you just as you are. Nothing you have done or will ever do can separate you from His love (Romans 8:38–39). Perfect, right?

If you have a hard time relating to this on a personal level, I urge you to get to know the tenderness of His love and grace. Think of God the Father and Jesus as the kindest, most tender-hearted loving ones you could ever be in relationship with. I used to think that God was a heavy-handed task master who played favorites. But that was only because my perception of Him was distorted. As you keep reading, you will find ways to overcome these kinds of misperceptions. When you truly understand and know this grace, your perspective will change. It is the immeasurable goodness of His love and grace that makes Him so attractive. It is what bids our hearts to draw near and love Him in return.

God's love is not only tender, but it is strong. Song of Solomon 8:6b communicates the tenaciousness of this perfect love: "For love is as strong as death, its jealousy as enduring as the grave" (NLT). Anyone who has experienced the death of a loved one can attest to death's strength. When I was twenty-four, my two-year-old daughter, Haylie Anne, suddenly died. Three months prior to that, my only brother, Charles (or as we called him "Midgie"), also suddenly died. The most dominant memory concerning those events is that death is so final. The strength of death interrupts and rearranges our lives with the same depth and intensity as a hurricane, earthquake, or tsunami—to the point that the landscape of our hearts and lives is unrecognizable. The Bible equates the strength of God's perfect love to the power of death. When we accept and ingest His perfect love, we will never be the same—our whole world will be completely rearranged.

If it is hard for you to receive or to give love, I want to encourage you to be intentional to know God's love. First John 4:8 says, "He who does not love does not know God, for God is love" (NKJV). First Corinthians 13 explains love so beautifully. This passage not only describes love but it also describes God Himself. If you need help with knowing this audacious love, please get to know these verses:

Love never gives up. Love cares more for others than for self. Love doesn't want what it doesn't have. Love doesn't strut, Doesn't have a swelled head, Doesn't force itself on others, Isn't always "me first," Doesn't fly off the handle, Doesn't keep score of the sins of others, Doesn't revel when others grovel, Takes pleasure in the flowering of truth, Puts up with anything, Trusts God always, Always looks for the best, Never looks back, But keeps going to the end. (1 Corinthians 13:4–7, MSG)

Read this Scripture in various translations. Read it silently. Read it aloud. Pray it. Meditate on it. Study it. Google it. Do whatever it takes to get the truth of this Scripture into your heart and soul.

We must allow the truth and depth of Jesus' love and acceptance to saturate our being and make it the foundation of our entire lives. I understand this may be a hard concept for some people. It was for me, and until I realized it, my faith life was rather precarious. I accepted Jesus as my Savior and asked Him to live in my heart, but I did not understand His tender love and His almost incomprehensible grace, so I compartmentalized Him. I gave Him a small place in my heart instead of trusting Him with my whole heart.

One afternoon while driving alone in my car, I did what I always do and poured my heart out to Jesus. I vividly remember His response. He gave me an example of the way I loved Him, and I now know He was trying to tell me my life would not have been so hard if I just would have dealt with my love issues.

Jesus showed me my heart and life as if they were a house. He told me I was content to make Him the semi-ignored room addition that sat off the back of my house. Then He made it clear He did not want to be the room addition—He wanted to be the house. In essence, He was saying He did not want to be just an add-on to my life; He wanted to be my very life.

I pondered this a long time, and I finally realized my love issues were fear and lack of trust, which caused a form of self-protection as I built walls around my heart. I wrestled with making Him the house, the Lord of my life, because I was too afraid to let go. Basically, I did not trust His love; I did not trust Him to do His best with my life. If we struggle with fear, then we can be certain we do not trust His love.

I am not going to try to sweet talk you into thinking heart hydration is effortless. It is simple, yes, but not effortless. However, falling in love with Jesus will change everything and make your efforts fluid—no longer mirroring a prison sentence. Grasping this perfect love causes all your efforts to make sense, empowering them with greater meaning. It is far easier to do something for love than it is to do it out of duty and obligation.

RELATIONSHIP—RELIGION—RULES

A lot of people are uncomfortable with the idea of having an intimate relationship with God. They think it is ill-mannered and that God, instead, should be worshiped and reverenced from afar. Some even go so far as to think He should stay out of their business and be there only when they need Him. But the Bible tells us in Exodus 34:14, "You must worship no other gods, for the LORD, whose very name is Jealous, is a God who is jealous about his relationship with you" (NLT).

Other people grapple with the idea of a relationship with Jesus because having a relationship with humans they can see is hard enough, never mind trying to have one with a big God you cannot see! This is totally understandable.

The best way for me to describe how to have a real, personal, intimate relationship with Him is first, just relax. He knows all about you and loves you despite your faults. You never have to try to impress Him—just be who He made you. Be yourself.

Second, set your heart to fall in love with Him. Determine to know His love and grace. In doing so, you will be compelled to love Him. If falling in love with Jesus is foreign to you, this also is understandable. But please, do not try to do life without it, for it is the core of life in Christ. Explaining *how* to fall in love is rather difficult. I mean who really knows how they fell in love? Most times it seems to happen without much planning on our part. The most valuable thing I can say about falling in love with Jesus is to surrender to His love. Just let go and let Him love you. Before you know it—you will be head over heels in love!

Third, treat this relationship as you would with someone you love and long to spend time with. Think about this: how much time do you invest talking, texting, and hanging out with the one you love? How much time do you spend thinking and dreaming about this special person? If you spent as much time with your spouse, family member, girlfriend/boyfriend, or best friend as you do with Jesus, what would happen to your relationship? Would you even have a relationship?

Thriving relationships require time, intention, devotion, and interaction, and if they are important to us, then we will give them everything we have. It is exactly the same with our relationship with Jesus. We cannot put Him in a box and simply visit when we need something. Our relationship with Him should be the source of our life.

Since we cannot visibly see or touch Him, we have to train ourselves to understand that He is always with us. Therefore, we must be intentional not to ignore Him and to practice living in His presence. Start this lifelong journey by establishing a designated time every day to read His love letter to you (the Bible) and to talk to Him (pray). First Thessalonians 5:17 says, "Pray without ceasing." Therefore, throughout your day, continue to carry on a conversation, and remember, it is a dialogue, not a monologue. Train your heart to hear His voice and to respond. Be willing to give Him the same attention you would give the person you love.

Those who struggle with the relationship idea just might have a religion issue. Why? Because relationship and religion operate at complete opposite ends of the spectrum. Relationship is birthed in love and grace, whereas religion is established by rules and control. I will be the first to admit, when it comes to relationship versus rules, rules are more inviting because they are less personal; therefore, you can engage but never really have to become vulnerable.

Choosing religion and rules over relationship is exactly what causes heart dehydration. Who can follow rules and succeed? This is precisely why we need Jesus. We can never be good enough or perfectly follow the rules of religion. Therefore, love on the cross made a way for us.

No one living for God can live by rules and not burn out or become bitter, controlling, demanding, and judgmental. When I was first working this out in my life, I used to work at being *my* best for God (religion), instead of just allowing Him to be His best in and through me (relationship). The Apostle Paul warned the people who wanted to live by rules and religion, telling the truth about living free:

Christ has set us free to live a free life. So take your stand! Never again let anyone put a harness of slavery on you. I am emphatic about this. The moment any one of you submits to circumcision or any other rule-keeping system, at that same moment Christ's hard-won gift of freedom is squandered. I repeat my warning: The person who accepts the ways of circumcision [rules] trades all the advantages of the free life in Christ for the obligations of the slave life of the law. I suspect you would never intend this, but this is what happens. When you attempt to live by your own religious plans and projects, you are cut off from Christ, you fall out of grace. (Galatians 5:1–4, MSG)

And in Galatians 2:21,

Is it not clear to you that to go back to that old rule-keeping, peer-pleasing religion would be an abandonment of everything personal and free in my relationship with God? I refuse to do that, to repudiate [reject] God's grace. If a living relationship with God could come by rule-keeping, then Christ died unnecessarily. (MSG)

Abiding in the grace of a relationship versus the duty of religion removes the heavy burden of working to be good enough for God and other people. It relieves the unnecessary tension of living for God, imparting peace and rest.

An important truth to remember is living in the grace of a relationship does not mean obedience is optional. Romans 6:1–2 says this about obedience: "Well then, should we keep on sinning so that God can show us more and more of his wonderful grace? Of course not! Since we have died to sin, how can we continue to live in it?" (NLT). We must know who we are—we have died to sin. We obey Him because we love Him. Scripture clearly tells us those who love Jesus obey Him, and those who do not love Him will not obey His teachings (John 14:23–24).

Jesus understands we are weak humans, and in our weakness, He makes us strong (2 Corinthians 12:9–10). This strength empowers us to live lives of purpose. Religion, on the other hand, will beat us down and try to disqualify us every time we falter.

Sometimes obedience in conjunction to relationship with Jesus is misunderstood. (I will discuss love and obedience with a lot more detail in chapter 8.) Our relationship with Jesus is grace and obedience based, not rules and performance based. Unfortunately, there are a lot of Christians living a performance-type lifestyle void of real relationship with Christ. Consequently, churches become dehydrated, weak, and irrelevant. In order for our churches to rise up, revival (heart hydration) needs to ignite in the hearts and souls of believers.

Before you move on to the next chapter, please take a minute to pray and ask Jesus to use this book to help hydrate your heart by bringing you into a closer relationship with Him.

2
KNOW WHO YOU ARE

A very important step in hydrating a thirsty heart is knowing who you are in Christ. If we accurately recognize who we are, and truly know who Jesus is in us, and if we really understand our position and authority in Christ, we will be able to hold our heads high, not in pride but in confidence of who we were created to be.

THE SIMPLE TRUTH ABOUT LIES

The truth about lies is that they just are not true. This sounds like a no-brainer, right? But unfortunately the main way the enemy of our soul (the devil) influences our lives is by getting us to believe lies about ourselves, others, and especially about God.

Lies sneak into our lives in various ways. It is important to understand that the devil will take every opportunity he can to lie to us. He has no regard for age, gender, or status and likes to take advantage of people when they are young or hurting. Some lies are subtle and slowly try to infiltrate our heart and soul. Other lies bring confusion by mixing with truth. And then there are the blatant lies that just outright falsely accuse.

The best way to fight and avoid these lies is to know the truth about who God says we are. Once we know and believe the truth about ourselves and about God, lies will be easily recognized and then we can appropriately deal with them.

Start by asking Jesus to give you discernment regarding lies, accusations, and deceptions so that every time they come, you can quickly recognize and expose them. The following is a quick and simple formula for addressing lies—use as often as needed.

1. Recognize
2. Exchange
3. Believe

In whatever way a lie comes, you must first recognize it as a falsehood, and if needed, repent for believing it. Recognizing a lie is rather simple. Essentially, you discern where the thought is coming from and what its purpose is. If it is from God, it will build you up, not tear you down. If it is from the devil, it will kill, steal, or destroy. Second, after discerning a lie, exchange it for truth. Third, adjust your faith and make the choice to believe the truth and live in its freedom.

THE EXCHANGE

To fully grasp the truth about ourselves, we must first realize who Christ is in us and what He has done for us. To completely explain who He is and what He has done cannot be told in this one chapter, or even in this one book. The most basic explanation is to see what He has done through the *Great Exchange*, which is summed up in 2 Corinthians 5:21: "For He [God the Father] made Him [Jesus] who knew no sin to be sin for us, that we might become the righteousness of God in Him" (NKJV). The life of Jesus was given in exchange for ours. This truth affects every area of our lives. Our brokenness was given in trade for His wholeness—we have been made whole—this is who we are. No matter what we face or what may seem to be lacking, the exchange applies.

Implementing the concept of exchange daily in our lives is essential and rather simple. Basically, whenever we struggle with something, we turn to Jesus and make an exchange. For example, if we are wrestling with rejection, we turn to Jesus and His finished work on the cross and make an exchange. We give Him the rejection in trade for acceptance. This practice of exchange helps us to remember the truth of what Jesus has done for us, reminding us of our freedom and who we are in Christ.

DEAD TO SIN

Because of God the Father's great love and because of our value to Him, Jesus became sin for us, and when He was crucified, in essence, our sin was crucified. He was raised to life from the dead and left sin in the grave. Jesus demonstrated His authority over sin and death when He was resurrected. Sin and death have no hold on Him. That is what makes Him a living God. Gratefully, He has given us that same authority, and now we are privileged to live a resurrected life.

Look at Romans 6 for a greater understanding:

For we died and were buried with Christ by baptism. And just as Christ was raised from the dead by the glorious power of the Father, now we also may live new lives. Since we have been united with him in his death, we will also be raised to life as he was. We know that our old sinful selves were crucified with Christ so that sin might lose its power in our lives. We are no longer slaves to sin. For when we died with Christ we were set free from the power of sin. And since we died with Christ, we know we will also live with him. We are sure of this because Christ was raised from the dead, and he will never die again. Death no longer has any power over him. When he died, he died once to break the power of sin. But now that he lives, he lives for the glory of God. So you also should consider yourselves to be dead to the power of sin and alive to God through Christ Jesus. (Romans 6:4–11, NLT)

One truth about living a resurrected life that took me a long time to understand was that I was dead to sin. I knew I was dead to my old sin, but because my sin nature was so strong, I wrestled with its struggle. Paul said,

Do not let sin control the way you live; do not give in to sinful desires. Do not let any part of your body become an instrument of evil to serve sin. Instead, give yourselves completely to God, for you were dead, but now you have new life. So use your whole body as an instrument to do what is right for the glory of God. Sin is no longer your master, for you no longer live under the requirements of the law. Instead, you live under the freedom of God's grace. (Romans 6:12–14, NLT)

Accepting the truth about a resurrected life is accepting a life covered by the freedom of God's grace. This can be difficult to grasp because our new resurrected life and our old sinful nature are always in conflict with one another (see Galatians 5:17). Paul described this dilemma:

The trouble is with me, for I am all too human, a slave to sin. I don't really understand myself, for I want to do what is right, but I don't do it. Instead, I do what I hate. But if I know that what I am doing is wrong, this shows that I agree that the law is good. So I am not the one doing wrong; it is sin living in me that does it. And I know that nothing good lives in me, that is, in my sinful nature. I want to do what is right, but I can't. I want to do what is good, but I don't. I don't want to do what is wrong, but

I do it anyway. But if I do what I don't want to do, I am not really the one doing wrong; it is sin living in me that does it. I have discovered this principle of life—that when I want to do what is right, I inevitably do what is wrong. I love God's law with all my heart. But there is another power within me that is at war with my mind. This power makes me a slave to the sin that is still within me. Oh, what a miserable person I am! (Romans 7:14–24, NLT)

When you read this, can you relate? You may be thinking, *So what is the answer?* The very next verse gives us comfort: "Who will free me from this life that is dominated by sin and death? Thank God! The answer is in Jesus Christ our Lord" (Romans 7:24b–25a, NLT). Again, this is why the answer to heart hydration is a relationship with Jesus. Paul went on to say, "So now there is no condemnation for those who belong to Christ Jesus. And because you belong to him, the power of the life-giving Spirit has freed you from the power of sin that leads to death" (Romans 8:1–2, NLT).

The Message version of the Bible puts Romans 8:1–3 so clearly: With the arrival of Jesus, the Messiah, that fateful dilemma is resolved. Those *who enter into* Christ's being-here-for-us no longer have to live under a continuous, low-lying black cloud. A new power is in operation. The Spirit of *life in* Christ, like a strong wind, has magnificently cleared the air, freeing you from a fated lifetime of brutal tyranny at the hands of sin and death. God went for the jugular when he sent his own Son. He didn't deal with the problem as something remote and unimportant. In his Son, Jesus, he personally took on *the human condition*, entered the disordered mess of struggling humanity in order to set it right once and for all. The law code, weakened as it always was by fractured human nature, could never have done that. (MSG, emphasis added)

I love how the sinful nature is described as "the human condition." Rest assured, the human condition is made right by Jesus, our love and friend Himself. As you read further, you will find ways to hydrate your heart and soul concerning the human condition.

HIDDEN IN CHRIST

Being defined by Jesus' resurrection also means that we are hidden in Christ. Colossians 3:1–3 says,

So if you're serious about living this new resurrection life with Christ, *act* like it. Pursue the things over which Christ presides. Don't shuffle along, eyes to the ground, absorbed with the things right in front of you. Look up, and be alert to what is going on around Christ—that's where the action is. See things from *his* perspective. Your old life is dead. Your new life, which is your *real* life—even though invisible to spectators—is [hidden] with Christ in God. (MSG)

The essence of being hidden in Christ is that He is in us and we are in Him. This is who we are; we carry Christ wherever we go. It is vital to grasp what this means. Because He is in us, we reflect Him. Jesus is the light of the world; therefore, we are the light of the world.

This is one of the most untapped biblical truths. I say this because if we really believed this, the world would be a completely different place.

Think about it. What happened when Jesus walked the earth? Love, grace, and acts of extreme kindness were freely given. The dead were raised, the sick were healed, and the broken delivered. The hopeless found hope. Darkness cowered. Jesus changed everything He encountered. This is our reality. Jesus said anyone who believes in Him will not only do the works He did but will do even greater works (John 14:12). This is who we are. *This is who you are.*

CREATED FOR A PURPOSE

I remember dropping my son off at baseball camp one day. He was the cutest chubby kid with glasses. As he stepped out of our vehicle, I said, "Remember, you are the head and not the tail" (Deuteronomy 28:13). He responded with his head down and in a low tone said, "I know." He did not sound convinced, but on the other hand, as his mom, I really believed it. I loved him and knew his potential. He was never created to be average; he had enormous value, potential, and purpose.

Whenever my kids left the house (to do only God knows what), my most common words to them were "Remember who you are." In my heart I knew they were not created to indulge in activities that contradicted who they truly were. I still pray and believe these words for them today.

It is the same with us. God fashioned us with great potential and value. He is that parent, our Father cheering us on, and in every situation where we are out of place or where we think we are unqualified, He is saying, "You are the head and not the tail. You are not average. You are approved. Remember who you are: you are loved, you have value, and you have purpose—more than you know." Our only job in all this is to simply believe this truth.

A lot of believers have identity issues. Because of the dysfunction of life, weakness to sin, the influence of the world around us, and the devil's plans, our identities can be stolen. When this happens, we tend to drift away from the truth of who we really are, leading us into living completely different lives than what God intended for us. Oftentimes, it will cause us to focus more on who we are not and what we do not have, pushing us into living a performance-based life of continually striving to be better and to get more.

Imagine a baby born into a very wealthy family who is stolen at birth by a poor family. This child grows up in poverty, never knowing who he really is, or what is actually available to him, and never knowing the deep love of his real parents. There are a lot of believers with this same problem. I was one of them. Not knowing who I was in Christ caused me to live under the thumb of oppression, never quite knowing the Father's deep love for me. Not knowing my true value negatively affected almost every area of my life. When bad things happened to me, I was not surprised. I truly believed that if something bad was going to happen to someone, of course it would be me. My relationship with God resembled that of a beggar on the street corner, a person who felt entitled, yet craved His pity. I prayed with a vague hope that He would throw out a scrap, because that was probably all He thought I deserved.

The problem with living this kind of life was that it was based on a lie instead of the truth. In the natural realm, it appeared I was born into less, but when I gave my heart and life to Jesus, all that changed. My new life is one of privilege, not entitlement. It took an awful long time to realize who I really am in Christ, but when I did, my perspective completely shifted and lined up with the truth, causing all aspects of my life to change for the better.

Once, while praying, I saw myself standing in front of a castle, waving a small sheet of paper at the rich owners who lived inside. On the paper was a list of all the things I wanted them to do for me (my prayers). I was desperate. With bare feet, I stood wearing a dirty, old dress and looking like a peasant. Suddenly, the Owner's Son came out and asked me what I was doing out there. He said, "You belong inside; this is your home." As I stepped inside, he took the list from my hand and said, "You do not need to wave these requests. All this is yours. You can walk hand in hand with my Father, lean your head on His chest, and simply talk to Him. You are loved. This is who you are."

This is who we all are. We were made for a relationship with God the Father, His Son, and the Holy Spirit. We are deeply loved. We are not neglected, hopeless people who have to stand outside of His presence and beg. We were made in God's likeness to know Him and live in His provided freedom.

The opposite of relationship and freedom is oppression. Think of oppression as a cruel and unjust master who holds a person's heart under the continual slavery of judgment, shame and condemnation. It breeds only fear and confusion, causing those who submit to it to forget their birthright.

Isaiah 54:14 says, "In righteousness you shall be established; you shall be far from oppression, for you shall not fear; and from terror, for it shall not come near you" (NKJV). When we read Scripture like this, we have a tendency to think that one day this will be our reality. But the truth is when Jesus died on the cross and was resurrected, this Scripture became our present-day truth. We are established in righteousness. Oppression, fear, and terror are removed from us, right now, whether we feel like they are or not.

For years, as I struggled with my identity issues, the Lord would remind me of Isaiah 14:4: "You will take up this proverb against the king of Babylon, and say: 'How the oppressor has ceased, the golden city ceased!'" (NKJV). I regularly prayed for my freedom from the oppression I was under, not understanding the cross had already freed me. We can save a lot of time and heartache if we will stop praying prayers that have already been answered.

Oh, but once I realized, by faith, the truth about the cross—the truth that Jesus has already accomplished everything, He shattered oppression and freed us from slavery of every kind—that was when the truth of who I am set my broken heart and life free. Galatians 4:7 says, "Now you are no longer a slave but God's own child. And since you are his child, God has made you his heir" (NLT).

We no longer have to live like an unwanted stepchild. We are heirs. We have complete access to all the promises in the Bible. They are not just words on paper; they are God's decree that tells us of our great inheritance in Christ Jesus. We have been established in righteousness. We are the righteousness of God in Christ Jesus (2 Corinthians 5:21). We are complete through Christ (Colossians 2:9–10). Ephesians 2:6 says, "For he raised us from the dead along with Christ and seated us with him in the heavenly realms because we are united with Christ Jesus" (NLT). He *raised* (past tense) us from our old, dead life just as He did Christ and *seated* (also past tense) us with Him. He has already done it. This is your reality. *This is who you are.*

I have had the pleasure of having many young adults who are not related to me live in my home. With some, I even went as far as to call them my adopted kids because in my heart they were. But none of them ever quite acted like my own kids do; they behaved a bit awkwardly and seldom made themselves at home. The truth is they never realized the access they had to my home or to my heart.

When it comes to a relationship with God, do not let this be your reality. Until you realize your position as a believer and follower of Christ, you will always settle for less and never realize the full access you have to the heart of God and to all He has provided for you. If you struggle to believe this truth about yourself, please do not beat yourself up. Instead, decide to believe it.

QUALIFIED

The enemy of our souls likes to stamp DISQUALIFIED across our forehead. Living under the burden of disqualification immobilizes believers. No matter where this lie originates within your life, you must know that it is a falsehood. The cross and the blood of Jesus stamp the word QUALIFIED across your heart, soul, and entire life. *This is who you are.*

In 1989 my husband and I had a life-changing prophetic word that gave us insight into our future ministry. But because my husband continued in his sin of adultery, and me in my sin of self-idolatry, *we* disqualified ourselves from what God had for us. We did this by believing the lie of the enemy that we were a hopeless case and could never be who God intended us to be. The heaviness of the lie burdened us with shame and condemnation. It got to the point where we hardly even remembered that prophetic word or who God said we were, and what we were actually meant to do with our lives. As the years went by, we figured we had missed whatever God had for us. If we had known who we were in Christ, we would have lived appropriately and not wasted so many years wandering in the wilderness of the enemy's disqualification.

When we suffer from identity crises, we allow circumstances, sin, lies, the enemy, and opinions of others to dictate who we are, who we will become, and what we will do. The truth is nothing, not even our sin, disqualifies us from who God has made us and for what He has created us to be. This is one reason why it is so important to know who you are in Christ and to live appropriately. Come hell or high water (of which I have had both in my life), we have got to recognize, own, and hold on to the truth.

Please take time to ask Jesus to help you believe the truth about who He is in you and who you are in Him. Ask Him to reveal any lies that you have believed about Him and about yourself. As He exposes falsehoods, please follow the formula mentioned earlier to deal with lies (recognize, exchange, believe).

3

STEP INTO IT

Heart hydration is accessed as we step into the fullness of Christ's provision for us. God, our gracious Father, has created us to be people who live a free and unrestricted life—a life that fully partakes of every benefit the cross has to offer. Would you say that you are living in the fullness of all Christ has provided for you? As you read the following story, keep your own heart in mind. Notice the similarities of this adult child's actions and compare his heart to yours.

A very wealthy man decided to give his only son—a most loved and cherished child, now an adult—a gift. It was not just a run-of-the-mill gift; this tenderhearted man wanted to bless his only child with an extraordinary gift. This father had worked hard his whole life and accumulated a great deal of money. He decided to give his son a mansion. Pretty extravagant, right?

The father let his imagination run wild. It would be an amazing house complete with extensive grounds, pool, pool house, garages, and a workshop. Not only did he find the perfect house but he filled it with everything needed to make it fully functional, comfortable, and nicely decorated.

The shopping took weeks to complete. All the while, the father kept his son's likes and dislikes in mind—he wanted it to be perfect. And it was. The house was the largest on the block in an extraordinary neighborhood. The father purchased the newest, most expensive and beautiful things anyone could want or imagine. The garage held cars, trucks, off-road vehicles, a motor home, and a boat. The workshop was fully stocked with every tool imaginable. Every single detail was taken care of; he even made provision for servants to care for the house and grounds.

Finally, the gift was complete, and he was ready to give it to his son. He felt a bit apprehensive about giving the gift. He did not want to offend, because his son was one of those self-sufficient types who wanted to do things his own way and without help by working hard and taking pride in his own accomplishments. His son might see the gift as too extravagant, thinking he did not deserve something he did not work for.

The dad made it a no-frills presentation. He simply put the house key in a plain box and sent it to his son. The enclosed card explained how much he loved his son and how he wanted to bless him with something beyond what the son could attain by his own effort. At the bottom, he scribbled the address and told his son he could find his gift at that location.

When the son arrived at the address, he was a bit puzzled and thought maybe the person who owned the house had the gift. He proceeded to ring the doorbell, and as he waited, he noticed a note off to the side. It simply read, "The key opens the door—step in." He unlocked and pushed open the massive door to find another note. It said, "To my most beloved son. I have given all I have to provide this beautiful home for you, and it is my pleasure to do so—it is all yours."

As the son explored the house and grounds, he noticed the attention to detail. It was everything he would have chosen. But he felt overwhelmed; it was too much. Did he really deserve such a gift that he had no part in attaining?

The son did not know how to tell his dad how he felt. So he just thanked him and moved all of his belongings over. But instead of living in the house, he pitched a tent on the front lawn. He felt he was not worthy to live in such a house, and besides, it was way too extravagant. But at least this way, he could admire and appreciate what his father did for him.

Unbelievable, right? The son was content to only admire the gift and never possess it. He was content to be thankful but never live in the house the way his father intended.

By now, you must realize this story is too ridiculous to be true. However, it will give you insight into your relationship with God. God, your Father, has purchased an amazing gift for you—the gift is the provision of the cross.

Beautiful Jesus, on the cross, made extravagant provision for you. First and foremost, He made a way for you to have a personal relationship with Him. If that were all, it would be enough.

Nonetheless, with a huge heart of generosity, He bought your salvation. He also provided unconditional, extravagant love. He liberally gave wisdom, grace, faith, tender mercy, victory, and boundless forgiveness. The cross purchased freedom from every kind of oppression and bondage, all fear, all sickness, all lack, all brokenness, and all pain from the greatest to the least—just for you. Regret, shame, condemnation, and guilt have lost their grip. When He said, "It is finished" (John 19:30b, NKJV), He meant exactly that. You never have to be ashamed—you are free.

These provisions are all yours, paid in full. The key is in your hand; all you have to do is possess it, step into it, and live in it.

STOP LIVING ON THE LAWN

Unfortunately, some of God's cherished children choose not to live in all He has provided for them. Some are satisfied to pitch a tent on the front lawn, content to just sit and do their own thing. Oh, they consider going in. I mean, of course, who would not want to take possession of it? But brokenness and fear keep them out, held in bondage, admiring it from afar, never stepping into this perfect gift.

Doesn't this sound absurd? Who in their right mind would pass up such an opportunity? All of us in some way have been or still are the son described in this story.

These actions fully describe the symptoms of a dehydrated heart.

I was just like the son. I loved God, loved Jesus, and tried to know Him, but fear and brokenness held me back from stepping into the fullness of the cross. Gracious Jesus used this story to demonstrate to me how I was content to only admire Him and His Word. He showed me how I kept my heart dehydrated by not stepping into all He had died to give me.

I would pray and ask over and over for Jesus to set me free from certain things. I wanted audacious faith. My heart, marriage, and body were in need of healing, my finances were lacking, and I had wayward sons. I wanted to know and live in this scandalous grace that I had heard so much about, and I wanted to live a blessed, abundant life!

Finally, my perspective changed, and I began to believe God's Word and take it at face value. It changed when Jesus said, "Step into all I have provided for you. Stop living on the lawn." Essentially, He was saying, "I am not going to the cross again. My sacrifice was enough—it is finished—you are free—I love you. You have faith, you are healed, you are provided for, you live in abundance, your sons are saved, you live by grace, and you are blessed. All this is already yours. This is my heart for you. Own it and step into it!"

This sounds a lot like what we read in the Bible, right? What you must realize is that faith, grace, the cross, and the Bible contradict what some may call reasonable thinking. First Corinthians 1:27 tells us, "The message of the cross is foolish to those who are headed for destruction! But we who are being saved know it is the very power of God" (NLT). This truth beckons you to come out of your box of logical thinking and courageously, by faith, believe the message of the cross. Faith always trumps what makes sense.

By God's sheer mercy and grace, I said yes. I was done coddling my dehydrated heart, and I chose to trust Jesus and His Word. I made the choice to get off the lawn of my relationship with Him. This decision, coupled with grasping the revelation of who I was in Christ, changed my whole life. I decided to step into and live in all He had provided for me.

When I took my first step into the house of His provision, my parched heart was immersed and overwhelmed. My thirst was quenched with the faithfulness of God. It was as if all the lights went on and I could see and understand the fullness of the cross.

Every want and need are met in Jesus. The only thing you have to do is to step into His generosity—step into the very heart of God for you.

Take a moment to examine your heart and life. Do you see signs of dehydration and places where you have pitched a tent on the front lawn of God's provision for you? Maybe you cannot even go as far as living on the lawn. Does the pressure of church, religion, rules, and expectations cause you to abandon the whole idea of living for God? If so, does that cause even more shame? Or could it be possible that you do not want to fail? Do you think your brokenness and weakness to sin cannot be overcome?

Maybe, you are apprehensive to live in His provision because you do not feel worthy of such a great gift. Perhaps you cannot get over your past. Are you that person who feels the need to pay for such an extravagant gift? If this is true, please know that the cross and all it provides is a gift, not because you deserve it or have earned it, and especially not because you are good enough. If you could purchase or earn this gift, it would not be a gift at all. What the cross has given can never be earned or bought, and we can never be good enough. Oh, thank God—Jesus is enough. Philippians 3:3b states this very thing: "We rely on what Christ Jesus has done for us. We put no confidence in human effort" (NLT).

The house in the story represents unearned provision where all your needs and desires are met. This is God's grace. The gift is the provision of the cross, the essence of grace.

Do you struggle to understand and live in the grace of God? Start by asking Jesus to renew your mind and change your heart about grace (more about this in the next chapter). The following chapters are intended to help you move forward in hydrating your heart and life to overcome what keeps you from stepping into the provision of the cross. Please be encouraged to step into all He has for you! You will never regret it.

4

THE "ME" FACTOR

At some point, we as believers realize that to quench our hearts' thirst and step into the provision of the cross, we just have to get over ourselves. When I was first confronted with this concept, I was embarrassed and reluctant. I eventually realized living for myself was not only shallow and superficial, but this kind of lifestyle also prevented me from knowing the truth about my identity in Christ. Therefore, I could never fully engage in a deep relationship with Christ, and my life bore little fruit. Romans 8:7–8 tells us, "Focusing on the self is the opposite of focusing on God. Anyone completely absorbed in self ignores God, ends up thinking more about self than God. That person ignores who God is and what he is doing. And God isn't pleased at being ignored" (MSG).

It is the kindness of God that calls for the surrendering of ourselves, the surrendering of what I like to call the "Me" factor. His kindness beckons us to stop being our own god and to put Jesus first, and in doing so, we abandon a life of idolatry—idolatry of what we want, what we need, what we think, what we feel, what we fear—idolatry of self.

That does not mean we don't need self-esteem. That would be counterproductive to knowing who we are in Christ. We need to believe in ourselves, in who we are in Christ, and see ourselves how He sees us, as approved, valuable, capable, and as *more than* conquerors. The Me factor is the part of us that is inclined to be prideful, loves to steal God's glory, and wants to be independent from Jesus. We recognize it in all forms of *self* issues, such as self-absorption, self-righteousness, self-centeredness, self-importance, self-interest, self-love, self-possession, self-satisfaction, or self-worship (pride). Self issues contradict a life of being hidden in Christ; therefore, they are a hindrance to heart hydration and need to be dealt with. Please understand that abandoning the Me factor does not mean our human condition will completely go away. I wish it would. How easy would that make following Christ? If only! What it does mean is that it will be put in its rightful place and will not be able to rule us.

To live a life where the Me factor does not rule, we must choose Jesus alone as Lord. What a privilege to live life where Jesus, by His grace and merciful love, leads and guides us. What an honor to live a Matthew 6:33 life of seeking God first: "But seek first the kingdom of God and His righteousness, and all these things shall be added to you" (NKJV). This means seeking first His kingdom and completely trusting Him and His Word. The kingdom of God is the rule and reign of Jesus in the heart and life of a believer. We will be identified and defined by what is most important to us.

Jesus' kingdom is His will. He is King and Lord in His kingdom. Seeking first His kingdom is seeking a relationship with Him above all else, pursuing Him not just as a savior or a genie, but as the love of our lives, best friend, and Lord. And if we call Him Lord, then we cannot contradict ourselves by the lifestyles we live. He is Lord over us, and who better can we trust than Jesus, who gave His life for us?

IT'S A HEART ISSUE

This kind of devotion is essential for living a hydrated, thriving life, but this is not what our hearts automatically default to. For this reason, we must continually seek a change of heart so we can step into living in this manner.

Let me explain. It would be easy to make a list of rules to follow. First, "seek Him," second, "be righteous," third, "make Him Lord." After making our list, we would religiously set out to follow the rules. But as previously discussed, living for Christ is not about focusing on performance or keeping a set of rules. It is about living in a relationship where our hearts *choose* to seek and love God. We adjust our hearts to step into living for Jesus.

Since our hearts are so easily distracted and do not always choose to seek and love God first, we must work on our hearts' attitude. This is a key component in the hydration process.

Most issues we face are not really about the issue itself, but about our hearts' attitude regarding the matter. Take tithing, for example. Most seasoned, Bible-believing people know what God's Word says about tithing and know tithing is not optional. Yet not all believers tithe because their hearts do not fully trust God with their money. So it is not really about money but about the person's heart attitude toward trust and money.

When we seek a change of heart, God in His faithfulness imparts a revelation of truth. A revelation simply means to suddenly realize something we didn't know or understand before. This truth, when ingested, changes the way we view and believe God and His Word. Therefore, it changes us in the depths of who we are—changing our hearts.

Seeking a heart change is as easy as turning to Jesus and making an exchange with Him. We give Him the part of us that struggles, and in exchange, we take back a softer, more willing heart and soul. As we do, Ezekiel 36:25–27 becomes our reality:

I'll pour pure water over you and scrub you clean. I'll give you a new heart, put a new spirit in you. I'll remove the stone heart from your body and replace it with a heart that's God-willed, not self-willed. I'll put my Spirit in you and make it possible for you to do what I tell you and live by my commands. (MSG)

This Scripture gives us so much hope. It helps us to see that our gracious Father will always assist us and make it possible for us to live by His Word. If at any time in life, especially while reading this book, you find your heart is hard or unmovable toward biblical principles, you merely need to check your heart and find out what your attitude and motives are. If you are being selfish, ask God to change your heart. Remember, where your treasure is, there your heart will be also (Matthew 6:21). If you are your biggest treasure and not God, your heart will not be pliable to changes that put Him first.

CLUTTER

The ability to seek God first is enhanced by removing the clutter that crowds our hearts, the obstacles that keep us from living in close proximity to Jesus, and the junk that holds us back from an intimate life with Him. The end result is a life set free of self and all the worries accompanying a selfish Me-factor lifestyle. Does this sound overwhelming? I know when I face a cluttered situation in my home, I tend to shut the door and ignore it because it is too overwhelming to tackle. Rest assured, as with everything else in your life, decluttering your heart can only be done through Jesus' grace and strength. Lean into Him and let Him direct you.

Clutter can include bad heart attitudes, an unsubmitted self-will, emotionalism, unbelief, offenses, unforgiveness, pride, bitterness, judgments, shame, wrong mind-sets, double-mindedness, self-limitations, self-disqualifications, labels, past failures, fears, independence (doing our own thing), and addictions. It also may include other things such as relationships, activities, hobbies, work, and ministry—things that are not necessarily sin but do crowd our hearts, and when given too big a place, they leave little room for a relationship with Jesus.

I would like to illustrate the problem with clutter with this story. In my house, when I am not sure what to do with something, I usually put it in the garage (much to my husband's dismay). Out of sight, out of mind, right? Well, almost.

When my kids were young, we drove a very big Suburban that fit the whole family. In Idaho, it is best to park your car in the garage during winter, so you do not have to scrape the frost off your windows every time you go somewhere. Well, our older ranch-style house had a very tiny one-car garage. Our massive Suburban and all the clutter could not coexist; there just was not enough room. In order to park in the garage, the junk needed to be cleared out. This meant my husband and I (mainly my husband) had to deal with the clutter. The stuff I did not want to deal with before now had to be removed.

Clutter crowds the important things out. Are you starting to get the picture? God wants to *fully* occupy your heart, so it is important to declutter it. Begin by first choosing to step into a lifestyle of submission to Jesus. (Decluttering concepts are made available to you throughout this book.)

Submission is usually something people oppose. It definitely brought conflict to my life. I like to call it the "s" word, because when people hear about it, they treat it like a curse word—I know I did. But that was mainly because I misunderstood its true meaning and value. Do not fret; if someone as strong-willed as I was can learn to love submission, you can too!

THE "S" WORD—SUBMIT

Submission is essential to heart hydration because it is about our relationship with Christ. When we submit, we are not giving ourselves over to a list of rules or to a heavy-handed task master. No, we are yielding to the authority of Jesus because we love Him and we have chosen Him to be our Lord. The truth is whatever we submit to becomes our lord. Why not faithful, kind, loving Jesus?

Submission is beneficial to the hearts of believers because it causes us to lay our lives down and draws us nearer to Jesus, helping us to display love through our obedience to Him and His Word.

You can always tell when somebody lives in the Me factor by their heart attitude toward submission. Why? It's because the Me factor (selfishness) wants ultimate power. Submission kills the Me factor in us; therefore, heart hydration transpires when we willingly choose to step into submission as a lifestyle.

You may be thinking, *Why? Why should I willingly submit? Why give up my rights?* I know that was my first reaction, and unfortunately, in my ignorance, I did not start to fully understand or live in the biblical truth of submission until after twenty-five years of being a Christian (twenty-five years is a really long time!).

Romans 10:3 says, "For they being ignorant of God's righteousness, and seeking to establish their own righteousness, have not submitted to the righteousness of God" (NKJV). Please do not choose to be ignorant of God's righteousness. Instead, choose to step into giving your heart, soul, and life over to Jesus as a lifestyle.

Living a submitted lifestyle does not mean living a life of perfection. Jesus is not expecting us to be perfect—just submitted.

When we view submission from the right perspective, it leaves no room for us to be bitter or offended at God. Instead, it just makes sense. God loves me, Jesus gave His life for me, He wants His best for me—I trust Him therefore I give Him all of me. Some might think living a life of submission contradicts living a lifestyle of grace and freedom. But that is not the case. Actually, it is just the opposite. In submitting we are accepting who we are in Christ and bowing to all the cross has provided for us.

Submission as a lifestyle needs to be rooted in three concepts:

1. It is about the *heart*—checking and realigning your heart attitude to embrace submission.
2. It is about *trust*—trusting that God is good and only has good for you.
3. It is about *love*—loving God with all your heart, soul, mind, and strength.

It is difficult to bow to God if you question His love and do not trust Him. Therefore, if you have an issue with loving God or being loved by Him, this should be addressed. Start by seeking a heart change, and as you keep reading, you will find various ways to deal with this lack of trust.

Quite often the concepts of surrender and submission are interchanged. Although surrender and submission are of equal importance and are very similar, they are not exactly the same. Surrender is what should happen prior to learning to live a lifestyle of submission or when you are struggling to relinquish something to God. Surrender means to give *up*. Submission means to give *over*. Check out these simple illustrations depicting the two:

- *Surrender* comes at the end of a struggle when we realize that we cannot handle things on our own, and we appear to have no other choice. We may try ninety-nine different ways to fix our life. Then, when we are absolutely desper-

ate and at the end of ourselves, we relinquish our lives to
God. We may or may not have a good attitude about this.
Sometimes, we are relieved to give up the fight, and other
times we are prideful and angry.

- *Submission* does not have to be out of desperation. It is an
  act of our will based on trust, just as a child willingly takes
  a parent's hand, not out of fear but out of love. The child
  may not want to be led but knows by yielding to his parent,
  he is at peace and can safely rest under his parent's authority. He knows he is loved, and even when he cannot see it,
  he knows his parent always has his best interest in mind and
  will do what is best for him. Submission becomes rooted in
  the innermost part of the heart.

When it comes to our relationship with God, we willingly *give*
Jesus our lives, trusting Him enough to hand everything, both big
and small, over to Him. We allow Him to be Lord.

Submission should happen daily, and it starts and ends with
humility. Please understand God is love. He does not desire to
shame or humiliate us. He is good and can only do good (Psalm
119:68). Humility is the opposite of pride and is our response to
understanding our position before an all-knowing, all-wise God.

SUBMIT AND RESIST

Let's face it. Because we're human, we gravitate towards living in
the Me factor. Submission is the best way I have found to deal
with the dilemma of my human condition. James 4 is my go-to
Scripture on the subject:

God resists the proud, but gives grace to the humble.
Therefore submit to God. Resist the devil and he will flee
from you. Draw near to God and He will draw near to

you. Cleanse your hands, you sinners; and purify your hearts, you double-minded. (James 4:6–8, NKJV)

According to this, humility and grace give us the capacity to submit. As we submit to God and resist the devil, he has to flee. Keep in mind we cannot resist the devil unless we first submit to God. This opens the door for us to draw near to God, and (I love this part) He promises to draw near to us. Furthermore, in this drawn-near place, we are positioned to give our hearts and souls to God to be cleansed and purified. We no longer have to live ruled by our sin nature but submit to our freedom as one who is an heir of Christ.

One of the best ways to start our day is to first pray and submit ourselves to Jesus. It is getting everything into alignment with His will. (Please note: you do not have to pray a daily prayer to live a submitted life. Submission is more of a heart issue, not a religious act. As for me I need to pray this daily because I need the reminder that I do not live for myself, and the Me factor in me needs the reminder that it is not in charge.)

As we come into agreement with Jesus, it helps us to recognize His faithfulness and our position as believers. It also is a good reminder to not fret or worry, but to remember that Jesus sits on the throne of our lives, and He has the answers to everything we may encounter throughout the day.

A daily submission prayer does not have to be a huge ritual. For example, every morning as I am starting my day, usually while making coffee or tea, I acknowledge Jesus and quite willingly give my heart, soul, and life to Him. I resist the devil, tell him to flee, and I draw near to Jesus. Simple enough. Later, I usually pray and submit everything to Him, praying James 4:6–8 over my husband, marriage, children, grandchildren, family, friends, relationships, pastors, health, ministry, finances, business, church—all cares and concerns.

Submitting to God and resisting the devil help set our hearts and souls on the right course daily. As a lifestyle, submission helps us to process the day-to-day happenings of life. Throughout our day, we can submit anything to God, whether it is a conversation or a situation. It sets us free from the devil's influence and oppression; therefore, it cannot be just lip service. Submission has to be genuine. After submitting, we then resist the devil and his lies, accusations, influence, and temptations, as well as our own attraction toward sin.

Resist is an action word and oftentimes requires more than just praying. Once when my mind was in a battle, I was bombarded by accusations about what certain people thought of me. I was trying really hard not to be offended, and I began submitting the struggle to Jesus. I prayed James 4:6–8, telling the devil, "I resist you and you have to flee."

All of a sudden, the Lord spoke to my heart and told me to go to the people I had the problem with and ask them to pray for me about my struggle. At first, I tried to tell myself this cannot be God, but as I kept praying, I knew it was (besides, why would the enemy ever want me to do anything good?). Ugh. My heart dropped. I was at a point in my relationship with Jesus where I was living a submitted lifestyle, and I knew not to question Him but to just obey. So I did. Humbling myself was an act of resisting the devil.

Sometimes, resisting the devil is difficult. In those times, we rely on God's strength and grace. We know God's grace is enough because we have followed the instructions in James 4:6–8 and humbled ourselves with submission. The devil is a created being and is subject to the Word of God. He *has* to flee when we use this amazing technique of submit and resist.

Thirty-Day Challenge: For thirty days straight, before you even get out of bed, turn James 4:6–8 into a prayer and give your heart, soul, and life to Jesus in submission. Throughout your day, remind yourself that you are choosing to live under God's mission for your life. At the end of the thirty days, take note of how you have changed. If this works for you, continue with it as a part of your lifestyle.

THE HEART AND SOUL

The heart is said to be the wellspring of our lives. Our hearts are easily distracted, and according to Jeremiah 17:9, "The heart is deceitful above all things, and desperately wicked; Who can know it?" (NKJV). Only God knows our hearts (1 Kings 8:39); therefore, submitting our hearts to Him just makes sense.

Furthermore, Ephesians 3:17 states that our hearts are to be God's home. Do you ever scramble to pick up your house before company comes over? I know I do! Living with the understanding that our hearts are to be God's home causes us to clear out its clutter and make room for Him. This allows for heart hydration.

The soul is essential to every part of our lives and is made up of our will, mind, and emotions. Psalm 103:2 tells us that our souls can be a little forgetful when it comes to the things of God. It says, "Bless the LORD, O my soul; and forget not all His benefits" (NKJV). With this in mind, submitting our souls also makes a lot of sense. Accordingly, we can see how important it is to not let the Me factor influence us. Therefore, I want to give you a quick overview of the best way to deal with the three aspects of the soul on a day-to-day basis.

The *will* is by far the commander and chief of the soul. If our minds and emotions get out of alignment, we can will them back in order. If the will is disjointed, it can persuade the thoughts and feelings to join it. When we think of a strong will, we often think of rebellion, but a strong-willed personality is not necessarily a bad thing because it will rebel against evil. A strong will can just as easily be used for obedience as it can for defiance. C. S. Lewis, in his book *The Case for Christianity*, said this about the will: "Free will, though it makes evil possible, also makes any love or goodness or joy worth having."

What is so interesting about God is He gave us free will. He did not make us robots who automatically fall into line, but we have the ability to choose what we will do with our hearts, souls, and lives. He will not violate our free will; it is His heart's desire that we choose Him out of love and not duty. This is where submission comes in. If our will is not submitted, it can quite comfortably live in the Me factor. John 5:30 says this about what Jesus chose to do with His will: "I can of Myself do nothing. As I hear, I judge; and My judgment is righteous, because I do not seek My own will but the will of the Father who sent Me" (NKJV). In living in relationship with Jesus, we are to imitate Him in all we do (Ephesians 5:1). If He did not do His own will, I am sure we should not either.

The *mind* is the center point of reason and thought. If left to its own devices and not submitted, it can absolutely run wild and wreak havoc. According to Scripture, our minds need to be renewed and transformed. Ephesians 4:23 says, "And be renewed in the spirit of your mind" (NKJV). And Romans 12:2 tells us, "Don't copy the behavior and customs of this world, but let God transform you into a new person by changing the way you think. Then you will learn to know God's will for you, which is good and pleasing and perfect" (NLT). Second Corinthians 10:5 makes this all pretty clear: "Casting down arguments and every high thing that exalts itself against the knowledge of God, bringing [submitting] every thought into captivity to the obedience of Christ" (NKJV). The action of renewing and transforming our minds, along with bringing every thought into captivity, is simply done by submission.

The *emotions* are where our feelings come from. Living according to how we feel is a very dangerous way to live. We should never allow our emotions to rule our lives; instead, we are to rule our emotions. When our wills and minds are submitted, our emotions will follow suit and circumstances will no longer dictate our actions and reactions. Some people (not you, I'm sure) think because life is difficult they have the right to live in the Me factor. They let their emotions rule them and are stressed, moody, overwhelmed, angry, rude, unforgiving, and have an overall bad attitude. The best news ever is when living a submitted lifestyle, difficult life situations do not determine our behavior—Christ does.

Emotions that are not submitted to Jesus can be very manipulative. Consider how children naturally use emotions to get what they want. Children will pout when sad, cross their arms when angry, throw fits in stress, and burst into tears at the first sign of opposition to their will. Let us not be stuck in childish behavior where the Me factor rules our lives, but let us grow in maturity by submitting our hearts and souls to Jesus. We have to be the light and share the good news. It is as my former pastor, Carl Tuttle, would say, "You can't share the good news if you're the bad news."

As believers we are grafted into Christ and have the privilege of living in relationship with the Holy Spirit. The fruit of this relationship is love, joy, peace, patience, kindness, goodness, faithfulness, gentleness, and self-control (Galatians 5:22–23). These character traits (fruits) are what guide our actions.

Through our mind, will, and emotions, the soul determines how offenses of the heart are handled. An un-submitted soul most likely will lead the heart to become angry and hard when broken or offended. With a submitted heart and soul, where Christ is already at home, heartbreak causes an immediate turning to and reliance upon God.

HEARING GOD'S VOICE

The Me factor is a great opponent to hearing God's voice. When self clamors to be first, we drown out Jesus' voice. As we step into submission and allow Him to do what He wills in our lives, the voice of self diminishes. As this happens, we can hear Jesus in our hearts and through His Word a lot clearer.

I used to really doubt that I could hear God's voice. I would waver and get anxious about it, never really trusting my ability to hear Him. As I fretted over this, I came to the realization that I *can* and *do* hear His voice. How could I not? I am in relationship with Him, and He is faithful to speak to me. The key is to put the Me factor in its place and believe that I indeed do hear His voice. It is more of a faith issue than a hearing issue. This is true for all of us. God is faithful to speak to us; all we have to do is believe we can hear Him and align our hearts to listen.

I love the phrase "practicing the presence of God." It comes from one of my favorite little books appropriately titled *The Practice of the Presence of God*, written by Brother Lawrence, a seventeenth-century monk who lived a sweet, simple life of vigor and submission to Jesus.

What does it mean to practice God's presence? This simply means we are to school our hearts and souls to find their joy in Jesus' companionship. It is being aware of His constant presence with us and choosing to walk in that reality—to step into having Him present in our lives 24/7. He desires to guide the thoughts and actions of our entire lives and all they entail: heart, soul, body, mind, and spirit. It is being in constant conversation, hearing, listening, and talking to Jesus. Practicing His presence is about a devoted relationship with the love of our lives that leads us to do all for Him with no fear of what people are thinking about us.

Think about this for a moment. In God's presence, we find and connect with all of His characteristics, such as wisdom, grace, peace, joy, love, forgiveness, faithfulness, power, help, protection, strength, confidence, companionship, and comfort—the list is endless. Why would anyone not want to live in His presence? To live this life of continual heart hydration, it is a good idea to choose to walk free of self.

GRAVE CLOTHES

When I first began to learn about the Me factor, the Lord revealed this human condition to me in a picture:

I saw multitudes of people. Each person was wrapped in strips of cloth (grave clothes). They were alive and breathing, yes, but spiritually dead. In addition to the multitude of people, I saw an enormous spotlight scanning the earth. God was searching His church, looking for hearts fully dedicated and abandoned to Him. The searchlight was God's presence, and when His perfect light shone on each individual, the apparel of death simply fell off. Dirty, stained rags were discarded and piled in front of each uncovered soul.

God was searching His church, searching for loyal hearts (2 Chronicles 16:9; John 4:23), pursuing the hearts of those who would make Him Lord of their lives. The grave clothes represented the life of self that kept people at a distance from God. It is important to understand the distance was not because God did not love them, nor was it because He was displeased with them. In fact, it was not at all about anything God had done; it was simply because they were too occupied with the Me factor. The searchlight of His presence was enough to free the spiritually dead from their grave clothes. All they had to do was let His glorious light fill them.

A lot of believers are wearing grave clothes soaked in the Me factor. They live primarily for themselves. One reason this is happening is because believers do not recognize their position and inheritance in Christ. Whether we want to admit it or not, if we wear the grave clothes of self, we can be the walking dead.

You may ask, *How can the church, God's people, be the walking dead?*

The bride of Christ, by the power of the cross, is adorned in beautiful, white wedding attire. Jesus' sacrifice accomplished everything, and we are free to live without grave clothes—that is a fact. The exchange has been made, but we must choose to walk in the provision of the cross. We dress ourselves in grave clothes every time we choose to be our own god.

We can cover our grave clothes with name-brand threads, and we can wear a mask to hide our gray, sunken faces. Sadly, we can go in and out of church, carry our Bibles, lead, serve, pray, worship, tithe, and even preach and pastor, but if we have little regard for a relationship with Christ, then Christianity is just a name and the church just a club where the life of Christ is void.

The church is not a building or a program. The church is made up of people who must *know* God—people with an undivided heart. If the devil can keep us focused on ourselves, he has us right where he wants us, fruitless self-seekers who never get to the place of knowing God or sharing His love.

As long as we live to please self, we are living in self-righteousness—dressing ourselves in grave clothes. In Isaiah 64:6, this righteousness is described as filthy rags. I know this is rather gross, but just in case the analogy of grave clothes is not vivid enough, pay attention to the biblical description of filthy rags. When Isaiah wrote these words, filthy rags represented used menstrual rags. This is pretty amazing and a bit disgusting. Our self-righteousness is comparable to used menstrual pads. I don't know about you, but these analogies cause me to want to step out of selfish living.

We need to realize the truth of who we are. We are the bride of Christ, adorned in pure white dazzling robes of His righteousness—not the walking dead clothed in self-righteousness (Revelation 19:8; Isaiah 61:10).

As you allow the spotlight of His presence to fill you, you will disrobe from the Me factor. Therefore, re-dress into an awakening of who He is in you and who you are in Him.

The good news is when we disrobe from Me-factor attire and empty our hearts of selfishness, we can invite God to fill us. Death to self is not the end but a new resurrected life. It is our portion, knowing He will never leave us or forsake us (Hebrews 13:5). He is always with us. He calls us to death of self, so He can live in us and we can live in Him. Galatians 2:20 states this boldly: "I have been crucified with Christ; it is no longer I who live, but Christ lives in me; and the life which I now live in the flesh I live by faith in the Son of God, who loved me and gave Himself for me" (NKJV). I love the last part of this verse: we live *by faith* in Jesus, who loves us and bought our freedom with His very life! This is great news. This is our reality! And if He then lives in us, we are more than able to handle life. Life can be hard. At times, it may even seem unfair, but God is still God and He is *always* good.

THE GRACE AND RIGHTEOUSNESS FACTOR

Another dimension of the Me factor is attempting to live the Christian life based on our own ability. This can be likened to living on the lawn of our relationship with Jesus. Living for God is not about the Me factor. The only part Me plays in the whole picture is our willingness to bend our wills to God. It is imperative to realize a relationship with God is not about what we can do, but about what He has already done, therefore about grace.

Another way to view grace is to see it as unearned, divine help and favor to walk life out as a follower of Christ. His grace fills in all our gaps. If we will say yes to this grace—step into it—it will make it possible to seek *first* His kingdom and live righteously. Please remember: righteousness was attained by Jesus on the cross, and we, His church, are the righteousness of God in Christ Jesus (2 Corinthians 5:21).

Since we are made righteous by the cross, why then do you think Matthew 6:33 says to seek His righteousness? Could it be because of our human, sinful nature? Is our human condition prone to gravitate toward unrighteousness? Is it because we tend to forget who we are?

The Me factor always pursues its own pleasure, an exact example of how we wrap ourselves in grave clothes. We are not to be discouraged by this but by *grace* seek first His kingdom and His righteousness, with the understanding that because of the cross, righteousness is already ours. We just need to realize it is ours and put the Me factor in its rightful place. We must grab hold of this truth and exchange the grave clothes for wedding garments.

As believers in Christ, we have the opportunity to walk in close relationship with Him. We never have to strive to be good enough because our relationship is not based on our goodness but on His goodness. Thank God for that!

Since Christ is our portion in life, we must take care not to become hoarders—storing up everything for self. One of the leading ways a stingy Me-factor life affects us is by keeping us from sharing our faith, hope, and belief in Jesus. Not sharing Jesus is one cause of heart dehydration and is the ultimate selfishness. We cannot be greedy with our hope and freedom—it is meant to be shared (1 Peter 3:15).

Please be encouraged to take your next step in heart hydration. Pray before you move on, and ask Jesus to show you the areas of your heart, soul, and life that are ruled by the Me factor. As He does, ask Him to change your heart and help you step into living a submitted lifestyle. As you continue reading, you will find ways to saturate a parched Me-factor-dominant heart and soul.

5

JESUS IS ENOUGH

I am sure you have heard the saying, "Jesus is enough." But what does it really mean? And how does it relate to heart hydration? Essentially, this phrase sums up the words in John 6:35: "Jesus replied, 'I am the bread of life. Whoever comes to me will never be hungry again. Whoever believes in me will never be thirsty'" (NLT). Food and water are the basic necessities of life; without them, you cannot survive. In this Scripture, Jesus is saying, "I am sufficient to sustain your entire life. Not just part of your life but I can take care of and fill your life as a whole. I am adequate and have met every need and want. You can apply me, my Word, and my provision to any and all situations in your life. I am enough."

HOW JESUS BECAME ENOUGH

In the summer of 2006, the words "Jesus is enough" became more than just a cliché to me. As I mentioned in the introduction, Jesus asked me after twenty-five years of marital unfaithfulness on the part of my husband to not divorce him. Instead, Jesus wanted me to change my heart, make Him enough for my life, and be a bridge that would make a path for my husband to find His unconditional love.

Submitting my heart and life to Jesus in this situation was one of the hardest decisions I have ever made. It was the biggest turning point in my life—a place of complete surrender. During this time, I had a constant vision of what my heart and life looked like.

I saw myself walking through a very dark tunnel with no light in sight. My hair was dirty and stringy. I was clothed in torn, filthy rags. My face was covered with sores and my head hung low. I was walking in a sewer and the ground underneath my bare feet was covered with countless pieces of shattered glass. Day after day, I saw myself trudging through this "tunnel of life."

Dehydrated. Devastated. Defeated.

Jesus, in His mercy, spoke to me, saying He was the *only* light at the end of my dark tunnel—the light I could not glimpse yet. I knew then I had to find Him. I had to look in a way that I had never looked for Him before. No more get-well-quick methods. No more self-sufficiency.

The dark tunnel represented the life I had made for myself. I knew *about* God but did not know Him. I did not know who I was in Christ or realize all the cross had provided for me. I did what I wanted, and therefore, my life was in darkness and despair. I needed to step out of selfish living and step into the light of doing God's will. Even what I was wearing in the tunnel—the filthy rags, the grave clothes of self—were a representation of the Me factor that I had dressed in for years on end. The Me factor had to be put to death. No more being my own god; I needed to trust Jesus alone. My head hung low represented the hopelessness of my heart. It was so broken, so dehydrated, that I almost believed it was beyond repair. I needed to trust my heart into Jesus' healing hands. The innumerable pieces of broken glass underneath my feet represented my shattered hopes and dreams. They were worthless and crushed, even the good things; there would be no putting them back together. Jesus was to be my new hope and my best dream.

I had come to the end of myself. Jesus alone had to be enough for me.

During this time (the darkest and most hopeless I had experienced), Jesus began to ask me some very serious questions. The first question was simple.

"Am I enough?"

I answered, "Yes, Lord."

Day after day, He asked, "Am I enough for you?"

"Yes, Jesus. You are enough."

Month after month, He asked me the same questions. "If I never did another thing for you, am I enough? If your life never got any better than this, am I enough? If you lost everything dear to you, would I be enough?"

I responded, "Yes, Lord, of course You are."

He persisted until one day, I answered truthfully. "No, Jesus, You are not enough. But I want You to be."

He was not angry with me. He only extended grace. This was the most pivotal moment of my life. The moment He had been waiting for. The moment when I, Regina Forest, would realize I could no longer be my own god. The moment that I began to turn from a performance-based lifestyle and step into a submission-based life in relationship with Jesus. Oh, thank God! I bet the angels rejoiced that day. *She finally got it!*

With that question being truthfully answered, Jesus then proceeded to ask even harder questions.

"If your marriage never got any better, would you still love Me? Would I be enough for you if your husband does not change? Could I be your husband? Would you allow Me to love you where he cannot? Would you love your husband for Me? Would you lay down your life as a bridge to him? Would you bridge his path to Me with your life and allow Me to be enough for you?"

I am not going to make this look pretty. Those questions crushed my heart.

"Jesus, do You know what You are asking of me?"

"Yes, my love, I do."

I wrestled quite a while with the reality of what Jesus was asking. It was then that He introduced a new word: *relinquish*. It means to let go. I was faced with letting go of the only way I really knew how to deal with life and letting Jesus be enough. I had to relinquish my rights, my will, my control, my pain, my fear, and my pride. I remember thinking two things: *I will just jump—I will put all my eggs into this one basket.*

And then I answered, "Yes, Jesus, I will make You my Lord. I love You and I will trust You and let You be enough for me." My shattered heart was in deep pain, not only from my circumstances but from the struggle of relinquishing.

It all boiled down to a trust issue. The crux of Jesus being enough is trust. Trust is what will allow you to submit your life to Him and make Him enough.

Making Jesus enough is a very radical move to make, but He loves you so passionately and so jealously. The cross is your example, and it will remind you that surrendering your life is a small offering in comparison. Jesus knows that trusting Him and letting Him be in charge is the best scenario for your life.

If you struggle with trusting Him, then please keep reading! The next chapter will help to strengthen your faith.

WHAT ABOUT "ME"?

Living a submitted life where Jesus is enough is all about Mark 12:29–31:

> Jesus replied, "The most important commandment is this: 'Listen, O Israel! The LORD our God is the one and only LORD. And you must love the LORD your God with all your heart, all your soul, all your mind, and all your strength.' The second is equally important: 'Love your

neighbor as yourself.' No other commandment is greater than these." (NLT)

For instance, when Jesus asked me to lay down my life as a bridge for my husband, He was saying, "Love me with your all, make me enough, and love your husband as you love yourself." What if the tables were turned and it was me who was stuck in the brokenness of adultery? What would I want my husband to do for me? How would I want to be treated? I would not want him to abandon me. I would want him to see my heart, to look past my sin and believe in me, to love me enough to see me through.

The loudest, most demanding question that most people face when loving others as themselves is, *What about Me?* I asked this question quite frequently when going through my trial by fire. I knew the Bible states that divorce is permissible when adultery has been committed, and I tried to use that as a way out of my marriage, all the while concerned only about my freedom, my happiness, and my relief. But Jesus responded with Matthew 19:8: "Moses permitted divorce only as a concession to your hard hearts, but it was not what God had originally intended" (NLT). Jesus made it clear that this was about my heart—not my rights. Besides, marriage is not a place where two people who have become one fight for their rights. Marriage is a place of unity and covering. (Please know I am not against people who divorce; this is just my story.)

Every time you find yourself wrestling to put others first, and the Me factor is screaming *What about Me?*, respond with these three, powerful words: Jesus is enough! It is against our human nature to love others as ourselves, and the only way we can succeed in loving so profoundly is to make Jesus enough for ourselves first.

ENOUGH IS ENOUGH

The word *enough* means sufficient to satisfy a need or desire. If you can really grasp and step into the truth of *Jesus is enough*, then you will always have what you need. You will never be lacking. This does not mean trials will not come your way but that your heart and soul will be full. Psalm 23:1 audaciously states, "The LORD is my shepherd; I shall not want" (NKJV). Think about this. The Bible promises when Jesus is your shepherd, you will not want for anything. Doesn't this sound inviting? The way this Scripture works in your life is by making Jesus enough. With that being said, I invite you to drink deeply of this truth, ingesting it—stepping into it—owning it—living it.

To live a lifestyle where Jesus is enough, we need to walk submitted to His love and His will in regard to *all* things, both big and small. We also have to purpose to make our hearts undivided and put all our hope and expectation *in Him alone*. For help with this, make the following Scriptures your prayer.

- "Let your unfailing love surround us, LORD, for our hope is in you alone." (Psalm 33:22, NLT)
- "My soul, wait silently for God alone, for my expectation is from Him." (Psalm 62:5, NKIV)

Prior to the questions the Lord asked me, the truth of Jesus being enough was introduced through my best friend, Cathy Brookshire. Over and over again, I would ask her to explain what it means for Jesus to be enough. As she would patiently explain, my heart began to respond to the idea. Jesus saw my willingness to make Him enough and met me there.

Sometimes, it takes time, a lot of time, for me to grasp and own things. One of the reasons I struggled with grasping the truth of Jesus being enough was because I was still living primarily for myself. I had no idea of who I was in Christ. The Me factor did not like the idea of losing its independence and having to become solely dependent on God.

HOW IT WORKS

Has God ever asked you to do something that you feel totally unqualified for? For me, it happens quite often. In these times, I find myself saying to the Lord, "I can't do it, but You can." This is the essence of Jesus being enough. It is as Paul said in 2 Corinthians 12:9a: "And he said to me, 'My grace is sufficient for you, for My strength is made perfect in weakness'" (NKJV). It is where we come up short that He makes up the difference.

To better understand Jesus being enough, visualize a rough surface covered with divots, grooves, and holes. Now imagine a large putty knife or trowel spreading spackle over the rough surface. All of the unsightly blemishes and holes are being filled in and smoothed out. In this same manner, Jesus completes you where you are lacking.

Another explanation (my favorite) is to visualize your heart in a dehydrated condition. Now imagine that someone commits an offense against you; maybe it is deep and painful or maybe it is just an irritation. See the offense as an arrow aimed and shot straight at your heart, piercing its depths and causing it to crumble. Now picture your heart after heart hydration. You know who you are in Christ. Your heart is now relinquished to Jesus and He is enough for you. You have stepped out of the grave clothes and into the fullness of the cross. You are walking in submission and you are recognizing and dealing with the Me factor.

Imagine that same arrow of offense coming again straight at your heart. This time, because you have hydrated your heart by making Jesus enough, the arrow hits but does not penetrate. There is no room in your heart for arrows of any kind, because your heart is already full—Jesus is enough. The arrows do not devastate you because Jesus is enough to take care of any situation that comes your way.

HOW TO KNOW IF JESUS IS NOT ENOUGH

A lot of people are not even aware when Jesus is not enough for them. How about you? Do you know who you are in Christ? When you read chapter 3 about stepping into the provision of the cross, could you relate? If you find yourself living on the lawn of life, just admiring God's Word and provision, then it is safe to say Jesus is not enough.

Examine your actions when hard times hit or when you are simply confronted by a rough day. What do you reach for? Comfort food? A friend to sympathize? The Internet? Shopping? Movies, TV, or video games? Pain relievers or antidepressants? Alcohol or drugs? How do you respond? Self-pity? Anger? Emotionalism? Taking it out on everyone in your path with a rude, nasty attitude?

When things got tough, I would close my door, shut my life out, and take a nap. This was one way I could avoid the truth. Other times, I would look for consolation by calling a friend or escaping with a good love-story chick flick. Reaching for anything other than Jesus in a crisis is a flashing neon sign that He is not enough.

Before Jesus became enough for me, my primary comfort was found in trying to be in control of my life. When a marriage issue came up (which there were many), instead of turning to Jesus, I turned inward to my anger and used cunning words to hurt my husband. Lashing out with manipulative, belittling words and a rude attitude made me feel in control. Once Jesus became enough for me, my heart changed toward my husband, and I could no longer find fulfillment in debasing him. I then started the practice of immediately turning to Jesus and asking Him to be enough for me, asking Him to meet me where the pain or frustration was and to fill that place with His love.

Another reality check is to examine your heart motives and pursuits. If your primary concern is for yourself or to acquire money, possessions, self-gratification, praise, status, and the like, then you can be sure these *things*, not Jesus, fulfill you. It would be fair to say Jesus is not enough.

Even the pursuit of God can be fulfilling in an unhealthy way. Pursuits in and of themselves are consuming, even if it is a ministry devoted to serving God. You can put all you are into the chase, but once the pursuit is over, you are left dehydrated because you were more driven by the hunt than the actual prize.

Being driven is good, but I am challenging you to hydrate your heart—to be driven to love and know Jesus more than *anything* else. He is the only pursuit that will not dehydrate you. When you make Jesus enough, your longing will cease and your emptiness will be filled.

Jesus is asking if He alone is enough for you. How do you make Him enough? You start by choosing to believe that He is enough. Be assured He will meet you right where you are—all He needs is your willingness.

6
FAITH IS ESSENTIAL

Hydrating my heart by hydrating my faith was definitely a journey. When I first became a Christian, I do not think I really understood faith. I prayed, but my prayers were more like throwing worries up to Jesus. I prayed and then went about doing what I could to fix things for myself. Faith in Jesus did not seem necessary when I could handle life on my own. Although I did not know it, I was my own god, and I was content to trust myself.

Trusting others was difficult for me since most of the people I loved acted in an untrustworthy manner, which made me afraid to be vulnerable. Because of this, I retreated to what I call self-protection. I built walls around my heart, soul, and life. Every heartbreak, betrayal, lie, and offense became the bricks and mortar. I built a secure fortress that no one could penetrate. The inside of this fortress was familiar and comfortable; it was a place where I felt safe, hidden, and in control.

But people who live in self-protection do not understand that it is a façade—it is not a place of protection at all. Living life in this manner damages us way more than it helps. Self-protection actually causes further hurt because it allows our hearts to become hard and bitter, keeping love and truth out, therefore keeping Jesus out. This is where becoming our own god and trusting ourselves creep in. The view from this self-built place of comfort causes us to see Jesus in the same light as we see those who have hurt us, forcing us to weigh and measure Him as we would the unfaithful. From this vantage point, Jesus seems untrustworthy. It is a very dangerous place to live.

One example of self-protection I created was when my daughter was diagnosed with a massive brain tumor. I prayed, our friends prayed, a lot of people prayed, and yet she died. I can only credit my daughter's death to the sovereignty of God. My pain and disappointment became bricks and mortar, and I built walls around my heart that accused God of being unfaithful. I still loved Him as best I could. I still served Him because it was the right thing to do, but in that self-protected stance, I would not give Him access to my heart, and I lost trust in Him.

Being completely unaware that I had built those walls, I did not really notice the skepticism that leaked into my heart. Then one night years later, while in a season of strengthening my faith in regard to finances, Jesus whispered, "I love you," and I uncharacteristically responded, "Then why won't you bless me?" The moment I uttered those words, my heart was grieved. I had accused Him. But I felt torn between truth and the emotions that wanted to hold on to that accusation. I was reminded of when I was grieving for my daughter, and I could not be where the presence of God was without uncontrollable crying. When I was in His presence, I could feel His goodness; I could feel His love, but there was tension because the walls of pain and disappointment would not allow my heart to believe He loved me.

Because I had not thoroughly dealt with my daughter's death, years later I found myself accusing Him of not loving me, just as I did when Haylie died, this time because I was struggling financially. What God was doing in that moment was helping me to remove the walls I had created when she died. He was using the financial situation to purge my unbelief in His faithfulness. He did this by showing me what was hidden deep within my heart, helping me to remove the bricks I had set in place all those years back.

Since I lived in self-protection, faith was not anything I thought of much, and I was comfortable with my Christian life until Jesus shook my world with His radical ideas of faith, trust, unconditional love, forgiveness, and wholeness. And I am so grateful He did!

Living a life with little or no faith makes for a very shallow existence and is one of the biggest causes of heart dehydration.

I know what it is like to be stuck in such a drought. Thankfully, by sheer mercy my heart was hydrated. It began by recognizing how steeped in fear I was. My faith was weak because I judged God's faithfulness by my circumstances. Real faith believes before it sees, based on God's Word alone. I failed to understand that the main characteristic of faith is that it attributes everything to God's Word—to His faithfulness and not to our circumstances.

Stepping into believing this way is hard for skeptical or hurt people. But one thing we must know is that Jesus is so patiently kind and gracious and desperately wants to heal our unbelief. He really does understand and will absolutely meet us, with open arms, right where we are.

The base definition of faith for a follower of Christ is this: we take God's Word at face value. When you have a twenty-dollar bill in your hand, do you ever question its worth? You probably do not, because on that bill it is plainly printed "twenty dollars." You believe what it says and take the worth of that bill at face value. Taking God's Word at face value is just the same. We read it and believe God is exactly who it says He is. Therefore, faith believes, without reservation, that God is faithful. It believes that He has done, and will do, *all* that is written in His Word, which gives us the opportunity to live accordingly.

Faith will get you from point A to point Z in any life situation. This is why thriving faith is essential to life in Christ and to quenching a thirsty heart. Hebrews 11:6a says, "But without faith it is impossible to please Him" (NKJV). In light of how important faith is, can you guess what the devil's biggest target is? Yes, the enemy of our soul is always out to steal or weaken our faith. I am determined not to let him! How about you?

How would you evaluate your faith? Lacking? Mediocre? Strong? Would you say it is dehydrated? Do you worry or fret? If so, then your faith is in need of being strengthened. Solid faith will catapult you out of a dry, wanting lifestyle and allow you to step into the truth of God's Word.

As you read further, please take an ensuing step in heart hydration by praying and asking Jesus for a revelation of His love and an invasion of truth regarding His faithfulness.

TRUST

Do you ever go to bed at night worrying yourself sick because you are not sure the sun will come up the next day? No, I am sure you do not, because that would be ridiculous. You probably do not worry about such things because you *trust*. Trusting Jesus should be just as effortless as trusting the sun to rise again. To understand the meaning of trust, let us look at its definition: confidence and dependability on the integrity, strength, and ability of a person or thing.

Trust is a necessary element of life. Without it, we cannot cross a bridge or drive a car, and it is dreadful to marry someone without trust. How could we go to work giving our time and energy to an employer without trusting they will pay us? It would be difficult to even go to sleep at night unless we trust we will wake up in the morning.

Trust is essential.

A hydrated life consists of many components—all requiring trust. First and foremost, we are to surrender and submit our lives completely to Jesus. How can we unless we trust? How can we know there is eternal life and salvation without trust? Reading the Bible would be difficult lest we trust its truth. Praying makes no sense—except we trust Jesus to listen and answer. How can we even believe in Jesus whom we cannot see if we do not trust He exists?

Trust is vital.

Faith is a response to our trust in God. Without trust, we will be faithless; without faith, we will be godless, and our hearts will always be wanting.

Trust is a choice.

It is easy to love Jesus because He is loveable. Yet loving Him and trusting Him are two different things. We must choose to trust Jesus to the point we can give Him our whole heart and life.

Understandably, trusting can be difficult for people with trust issues, but nonetheless, the choice is ours. To live in relationship with Jesus, we must choose to trust Him and to believe His Word.

When we deal with our trust issues, all of our relationships, especially our relationship with God, will flourish. Let us be the kind of people who trust Jesus just as much as we trust the sun to come up tomorrow.

UNBELIEF AND TRUE FAITH IN GOD

I have to say the simplicity and complexity of faith in God and His Word often perplexed me. The reason for the bewilderment admittedly was unbelief and the underlying factor of fear in my life. The enemy of my soul, combined with harsh life situations, continually tried to steal my faith.

It is imperative to understand how deadly unbelief is in the heart of a believer; it is a cancer that must be ruthlessly dealt with because it will devour all hope and cause those desiring to live for God to be unable to enter into an intimate relationship with Him. Please do not allow yourself to be an unbelieving believer.

There are predominantly two kinds of Christians: the ones who go through life's sufferings with grace—allowing every trial to strengthen them, and those who go through life hardship after hardship—just weathering each storm. The reason people live the "hunker down and get through it" kind of life is because they fail to see the real problem. It is not the hardships they face but their lack of true faith in God. I know this because it was my experience.

The Lord first began to heal my unbelief through a relationship with a dear friend and mentor, Wilma Dee Benson, an eighty-two-year-old woman of wisdom. I met Wilma right around the time my life fell apart. She knew the importance of strong faith and continually challenged me in this area. One topic of discussion was regarding Mark 11:20–24:

> In the morning, as they went along, they saw the fig tree withered from the roots. Peter remembered and said to Jesus, "Rabbi, look! The fig tree you cursed has withered!"
> "Have faith in God," Jesus answered. "Truly I tell you, if anyone says to this mountain, 'Go, throw yourself into the sea,' and does not doubt in their heart but believes that what they say will happen, it will be done for him. Therefore I tell you, whatever you ask for in prayer, believe that you have received it, and it will be yours. (NIV)

Wilma insisted on giving me a copy of a message preached by David Wilkerson on this Scripture. I was reluctant to hear yet another message on mountain-moving faith. I was tired of hearing about moving the mountains of trouble in my life because they never seemed to budge but continued to stand looming over me.

In time, I began to realize the reason they would not shift was not because of God's unfaithfulness but because of my unbelief. I am really glad Wilma persisted because the message spoke volumes to my heart, helping me to see this Scripture a little differently, and most importantly to see the truth about unbelief.

Wilkerson's message echoed the truth about the mountains we face. A troubled marriage, finances, rebellious children, depression, addictions, impossible circumstances, grief, illness—depending on our faith—feel as enormous as Mt. Everest. But in reality, these seemingly hopeless situations are not our biggest issue.

The mountain we face is unbelief.

Everything in life that presents itself as a mountain originates from unbelief. Therefore, if we have true unwavering faith in God, there will not be mountains to face because true faith in God believes He is bigger than circumstance, bigger than any problem or trial that tries to rise against us.

True faith in God does not worry or fret wondering if God will perform. True faith in God knows He can and will come through. True faith in Jesus rests confidently in His will, His Word being done, and does not try to manipulate Him to do what we want Him to do.

We have got to love this! The mountains we face are not objects of opposition at all. The mountain is what is in us; it is what we believe or do not believe about Jesus and the Word of God.

Years later, I began to understand Mark 11:24, where Jesus said, "Therefore I say to you, whatever things you ask when you pray, believe that you receive them, and you will have them" (NKJV). Essentially, Jesus is saying when you have true faith in God, you must believe that you have received—right after asking, then you will have what we asked for. For some, this goes against the grain of how you believe. But truth is truth, and the truth of this Scripture is you have to believe you will receive anything you ask for before you actually see it. Appropriating your faith to believe in this manner changes your life! It certainly changed my life.

The issue of unbelief, no matter how small or how large, must be addressed. Start by finding out what resides inside your heart and soul that prevents you from stepping into believing, and then ask Jesus to heal your unbelief. Mark 9:21–24 is a great example. In this Scripture, the man brought his demon-possessed son to be healed. We see that he had faith enough to come to Jesus, but he wavered in unbelief.

> So he [Jesus] asked his father, "How long has this been happening to him?" And he said, "From childhood. And often he [the evil spirit] has thrown him both into the fire and into the water to destroy him. But if You can do anything, have compassion on us and help us." Jesus said to him, "If you can believe, all things are possible to him who believes." Immediately the father of the child cried out and said with tears, "Lord, I believe; help my unbelief!" (NKJV)

His unbelief is recognized by the word *if*. He said to Jesus "if You can." I love Jesus' response. He turned the responsibility over to the man by saying it was up to him. *If* he could step out of unbelief, then his faith would make his child well. How many times do we use such a faithless word as *if?* What Jesus said next is amazing! He said, "Everything is possible for him who believes." Then the man came to his senses and said, in essence, "Yes, I believe, but please, Jesus, heal the part of me that is struggling with unbelief—heal my weak faith." If you vacillate in your faith, then this, no doubt, should be your prayer.

The benefit of true faith in God, besides heart hydration, is that "everything is possible for him who believes." *Everything* according to the Word of God is possible for us who believe! This is really good news! Just this truth alone should cause us to desire true, strong, unwavering faith.

GOD'S WORD IS HYDRATION

A very important issue that must be settled in order to have true faith in God is in this question: what are we basing our belief system on? If our answer is anything other than the Bible, we will always have a divided heart and mind, two major enemies to trusting God.

Romans 10:17 informs, "So then faith comes by hearing and hearing by the word of God" (NKJV). *Reading the Bible is a crucial way to attaining true faith in God and therefore heart hydration.*

If we call ourselves believers, then we have to believe the Word of God is the only truth. There are no half-truths when it comes to believing in God and His Word. Either it is the truth or it is not. We must determine to base our belief system on the Bible, God's divine Word, using it as our plumb line, the *only* truth and guide for everything in life. The Bible is not something we casually read nor is it something we just admire.

Embrace the truth that God's Word is Jesus Himself (John 1:1, 14). Embracing His Word draws you into a closer relationship with Him. God's Word is hydration. It is alive and active (Hebrews 4:12; Psalm 33:6, 9). When ingested it cleanses, comforts, heals, delivers, forgives, and creates. The Word brings life to every thought and situation it touches.

One tangible way to daily hydrate our hearts and souls is what I call "Word in, Word out." It is as uncomplicated as it sounds. Put the Word of God in and speak it out. For example, when I was dealing with sickness, I wrote healing Scriptures on my bathroom mirror. Instead of wasting my thoughts on my symptoms, every time I saw the Scripture, I would read it and speak it to my body. I would say it out loud and affirm its truth to my heart and soul. It is beneficial to practice Word in, Word out daily because we need God's truth to be our truth.

When we take the Word in, we are in essence taking in the presence of God, inhaling Jesus Himself. And when we speak it out, we are breathing the life of God into every situation with our very words. So not only does it change who we are, but it speaks life to all who are around us.

Most importantly, this concept increases our faith. As we speak it, our ears hear it, and our minds begin to believe it. Instead of letting our thoughts run wild or consume us, we use our idle thought time to take the Word in and speak it out.

Another good method of application is to write a Scripture on a note card or sticky note and post it where you will see it. Every time you see it, read it out loud and speak it to your heart and soul.

As you put the Word in and speak it out, remember to believe it. Believe the truth, the truth that it cannot enter your heart and soul without creating change and imparting hope—hope that then changes your perspective, causing you to see the beauty of your life through the eyes of Jesus.

> *Thirty-Day Challenge:* I challenge you to apply the "Word in, Word out" concept to your life for thirty days straight and see how it changes your faith. Write a Scripture on a note card or sticky note and post it where you will see it. Every time you see it, read it out loud and speak it to your heart and soul. Do you accept the challenge?

GOD'S FAITHFULNESS IS NOT IN QUESTION

When I struggled to trust God, it was mainly because I was fearful of being hurt and disappointed. This is a very tough place to live in and difficult to break out of because it begins with a step of faith. The very thing we need is faith, and faith is the very thing that will get us what we need. Romans 12:3 tells us everyone has faith inherent within them. Therefore, to move from not trusting God to trusting Him, we have to do what Peter did when he walked on the water (Matthew 14:27–31). We need to set fear aside and say yes to Jesus' call and step out of the boat!

The bottom line is that God's faithfulness is not in question, nor should it ever be. From the pulpit I've heard this fact communicated with the words, God's faithfulness is not on trial. Ponder this statement for a minute. We never have to figure out whether or not He will act faithfully.

God is faithful.

If we are to move the mountain of unbelief out of our lives, then beyond a shadow of doubt, we must settle this truth in our hearts and souls. We have to reset our core belief, and the truth about who God is must be our foundation. The primary truth about God is that He is always good. Psalm 100:5 shouts this truth: "For the LORD is good; His mercy is everlasting, and His truth endures to all generations" (NKJV). It is imperative to set this as the default truth we believe about God. When Psalm 100:5 is our bottom line, we will not waver in the face of hardships. Instead, we will know God is good, no matter what we face.

This certainty also helps if we struggle with the fear of disappointment. Sometimes, we are too afraid of being disappointed to even ask God for anything. Instead, we try to work out life on our own, and we all know how those scenarios end!

But if at the very core of our belief system, we know God is good, then fear of being disappointed will have no grip. Instead, we will rest and know God is faithful to His Word. Rather than worrying or focusing on our circumstances, our part is simply to draw near to God, stand firm, wait, and focus on Him and His faithfulness. He will do the rest.

If we ever have suspicion regarding His faithfulness, it is not God who needs to be questioned. Quite the contrary, we have only to look at our own hearts, questioning ourselves about *our* unbelief. No matter what has or has not happened in the past, it is essential to take God at His Word.

God continuously comes through, maybe not always in our timing or with what we want, but He does come through. I know there are times when we cannot see or feel God's faithfulness, but that does not contradict the truth about who He is. How do I know this? Because it is written in the Bible in Numbers 23:19: "God is not a man, so he does not lie. He is not human, so he does not change his mind. Has he ever spoken and failed to act? Has he ever promised and not carried it through?" (NLT).

Is there anyone so faithful? Humans lie and change their minds, and humans disappoint. God never does—the Bible plainly tells us. And since we have *chosen* to base our belief system on the Bible, we believe this to be true.

The Bible also says Jesus never changes or casts a shifting shadow (James 1:17). His Word is right and true; He is faithful in all He does (Psalm 33:4).

EXPECTATION

Not only do we need to believe in God's faithfulness, but we also need to live with the expectation of His faithfulness, not in entitlement, but where we simply expect Him to be faithful to His Word. While learning this, I experienced a crisis of belief that helped me change my expectations of God.

One extremely cold and windy spring morning, I was at my son's soccer game. I was working on thanking Jesus for the weather and heard Him say, "Why don't you ask me to stop the wind?"

So I did. I asked Him to please stop the wind. After praying, I looked around, somewhat waiting for it to stop. When it did not, I just shrugged. I got what I expected—nothing.

Then my older son, who was hunkered down next to me, asked, "Why don't you ask God to stop the wind?"

I responded, "I did."

What he spoke next stabbed deeply, as if God Himself were asking. He said, "Did you believe it when you asked?"

I truthfully had to say no.

My crisis of belief was I did not even *expect* God to answer. I just routinely asked Him, as if it were my Christian duty. It was true, double-minded lip service, not wholehearted belief.

Not expecting God to answer our prayers is unbelief. Expecting Him to be faithful reinforces our trust in Him. Faith-filled believers pray *according to His Word* with confidence of who He is, expecting nothing less than what He has promised, expecting nothing less than for Him to respond faithfully.

We must live expecting God to be faithful. It is essential to know and trust the truth that *it is against God's character to be unfaithful.* Say this aloud to yourself. Make this statement your bottom line about God.

Another thing that has helped boost my faith and expectation in God is done before I pray. I remind myself what the Word of God says in 1 John 5:14–15, then I confidently thank Him for hearing me and for answering my prayers: "This is the confidence we have in approaching God: that if we ask anything according to his will, he hears us. And if we know that he hears us—whatever we ask—we know that we have what we asked of him" (NIV).

WITHOUT WAVERING

What has God's Word promised? What has God's Word promised *you* personally?

The entire Bible is promise after promise. Ask yourself this question, *Am I fully convinced that God will do all He has promised?* Can you answer yes to this question without wavering? Wavering is defined as being unsteady, doubting, being indecisive, and being double-minded. Listen carefully to how James 1:6–8 describes wavering: "But let him ask in faith, with no doubting, for he who doubts is like a wave of the sea driven and tossed by the wind. For let not that man suppose that he will receive anything from the Lord; he is a double-minded man, unstable in all his ways" (NKJV).

This Scripture tells us that if we are not absolutely confident that God will do what we ask (according to His Word), then we are unstable in all our ways. This is serious business! A dehydrated heart can be equal to being unstable in all our ways. And since we are determined to live thriving, hydrated lives, we cannot be halfhearted but rather fully convinced that God will do all He has promised.

Romans 4:20–22 illuminates this very truth: "He [Abraham] did not waver at the promise of God through unbelief, but was strengthened in faith, giving glory to God, and being fully convinced that what He had promised He was also able to perform. And therefore it was accounted to him for righteousness." In the life of a believer, vacillating, casual faith should not exist. It is imperative we be fully convinced of His faithfulness, fully convinced that He always keeps His promises. Psalm 145:13b says, "The LORD always keeps his promises; he is gracious in all he does" (NLT). We need to choose to be the kind of people who believe without doubting.

But how can we be fully convinced, without wavering, that God will do all He has promised? The answer to this question is very obvious but one we frequently overlook. We can be sure God will fulfill every promise because the truth is God *has already* fulfilled every promise. Jesus Himself is the promise through His finished work on the cross—in Him every need is met. Again, that is why the key to heart hydration is a relationship with Jesus.

It is difficult to believe this way because in our human condition, we too often rely on our feelings instead of the truth of God's Word. For example, in the Bible, we see that Jesus heals the sick, and we read the Scripture, "And by his wounds we are healed" (Isaiah 53:5b, NIV). Where the wavering comes in is when we still *feel* sick. Our feelings cause us to be tossed back and forth, thinking, *Well, I guess Jesus didn't want to heal me.* With this kind of thinking, what we do not realize is that we are accusing Jesus of lying. Another example is the Scripture Philippians 4:19: "And my God shall supply all your need according to His riches in glory by Christ Jesus" (NKJV). We waver when the things we assume are needs are not met. With our wrong perspective, we accuse God of not being faithful by questioning, *Surely, God, this is a need. Why aren't you supplying the money I need to meet it?* Truth be told, if it were a need, He would have supplied it. He *always* meets our needs.

Standing on the Word of God is essential (Ephesians 6:10–19). To stand on the Word of God is to make a decision to believe, without wavering, the truth of the Word instead of our thoughts, circumstances, or feelings. In a sense, we plant our feet and determine not to be moved. Standing on God's Word can be a struggle because the devil, our culture, and the Me factor will always try to pull our feet out from under us and cause us to question God's faithfulness. This is why we must be fully convinced and determined to stand.

STRENGTHEN YOUR FAITH

How do we move from halfhearted belief to being fully convinced? Again, Romans 4:20–21 says, "[1] He [Abraham] did not waver at the promise of God through unbelief, [2] but was strengthened in faith, [3] giving glory to God, and [4] being fully convinced that what He had promised He was also able to perform" (NKJV).

The following are ways to apply Romans 4:20 and strengthen your faith. Please do not religiously go through the list below. Instead, prayerfully read it and let Jesus show you what applies to you.

1.   Do not waver in unbelief.
   • Determine to trust and believe God. (Proverbs 3:5)
   • Take a step of faith toward believing. (Matthew 14:27–31)
   • Know the truth of God's Word. (John 8:32)
   • Choose to stand on the truth of God's Word. (Ephesians 6:10–19)
   • Choose heart hydration. (Isaiah 44:3)
2.   Allow your faith to be strengthened.
   • Repent and ask for forgiveness for unbelief. (Acts 3:19)
   • Submit your unbelief to God and resist the devil. (James 4:7)
   • Draw near to God. (James 4:8)
   • Pray for deliverance from a spirit of unbelief. (Psalm 34:17)
   • Ask God to heal unbelief. (Mark 9:24)
   • Exchange unbelief for faith. (Isaiah 53:3–6; Galatians 3:13–14)
   • Ask God for a change of heart regarding trust and faith. (Ezekiel 36:26)
   • Read, hear, speak, and obey the Word of God. (James 1:22–25; Romans 10:17)

- Read and meditate on faith Scriptures. (Hebrews 11)
- Live a life of worship. (Luke 4:8)
- In everything give thanks. (1 Thessalonians 5:18)
- Fast and pray. (Mark 9:29)
- Invite the Holy Spirit into the empty place of unbelief in your heart and life. (Galatians 5:22–25)
- Wait on the Lord. (Psalm 27:14)
- Attend, serve, and be a part of a local church where your faith is stirred. (Ephesians 3:9–11; Hebrews 10:25)
- Tithe and decide to trust God with your money. (Malachi 3:8; Matthew 6:21)

3. Give glory to God.
   - Deal with pride. (James 4:6)
   - Humbly acknowledge God in your life, giving Him glory for everything. (John 7:18)

4. Be fully convinced that what He has promised He is able to perform.
   - Train your heart, mind, will, and emotions to trust God's faithfulness. (Deuteronomy 7:9)
   - Resolve to believe that unfaithfulness is against God's character. He cannot be unfaithful. (2 Timothy 2:13)

Pray and ask what steps you should take—then take those steps!

DO NOT WASTE THE WAIT

Even those with the strongest faith come up against *the wait*. The wait is that beautiful time in between promise and fulfillment. The wait is inevitable. And it can seem contradictory to living a faith-filled life where we take God's Word at face value and believe the cross accomplished everything. Our natural minds might think, *If Jesus fulfilled every promise, then why do I have to wait for it to come to me personally?* This is another area where my faith wavered.

I used to pray and ask God for things according to His Word, and when I did not see it, I thought He had not answered. I could not understand that faith is believing before you see—I wanted to see and then believe. Because my faith wavered, I continually asked the Lord, "What closes the gap between promise and fulfillment?" His answer to my question was "faith." Faith is the substance (Hebrews 11:1) that closes the gap between promise and fulfillment. True faith in God causes us to believe His Word and to stop weighing the truth of His Word against our circumstances and feelings. In essence, if we will only believe God's Word, the time between promise and fulfillment will no longer appear as a huge cavern. Instead, faith will fill in the gap, and we will spend the waiting period standing on God's Word, looking with expectancy for the fulfillment.

The problem is who loves to wait? When was the last time you waited and, without sarcasm, gave thanks for it? We live in an "I want it now" society. Our culture has trained us not to wait, and most of the time, waiting feels like a punishment.

It is very important to view waiting as valuable. If it were not beneficial for us, God would not allow it. Waiting will affect us either positively or negatively. Why not allow it to etch beauty on our hearts, therefore hydrating our lives?

We first start by asking God to change our hearts in regard to waiting. Seeking a heart change will help us yield to the process. Fighting the waiting process opens many doors, namely bitterness and unbelief. Second, we need to ask God about what He wants to accomplish in us during the waiting period.

The waiting phase between promise and fulfillment is easy to squander. We can easily waste it by engaging in fear and worry. Fear is the opposite of faith and the devil's biggest tactic against us. Remember, our enemy is always out to steal our faith, trying to make us unbelievers. If he can steal our faith, he will steal our destiny and our purpose. Fear is a thief and will ever so quickly throw us into the arms of worry.

Worry is horrific! The literal definition is to seize by the throat and repeatedly bite, shake, and mangle. Yes, that is the meaning of worry—oh, I know that one! Worry is also defined by the words anxiety, torment, devour, and harass. No wonder Jesus in Matthew 6:25–34 tells us not to worry. Listen to the warning about worry in Philippians 4:6–7: "Don't worry about anything; instead, pray about everything. Tell God what you need, and thank him for all he has done. Then you will experience God's peace, which exceeds anything we can understand. His peace will guard your hearts and minds as you live in Christ Jesus" (NLT).

Notice that according to verse 6, we are to pray and then immediately thank God for the answer. This is the kind of faith that closes the gap between promise and fulfillment. Once we have prayed and asked God to answer according to His Word, seal the deal with a thankful heart attitude. This tells God and our own hearts that we know He will be faithful to His Word. Thankfulness is our evidence of things not yet seen. It keeps us correctly focused so that we do not wander into worry.

Here are some truths about waiting that will help us not waste the wait:

- Waiting does not change the truth about God. He is still faithful.
- There is beauty in the waiting process. We just need to look for it.
- Waiting brings change. We can let it change us for the better.
- No matter what season we are in, waiting will play a part. Expect it.
- Embrace the wait. This will ease the pain of waiting.

- Waiting is not an interruption to God's will. Do not try to avoid it.
- Waiting diminishes self-absorption. We discover it is not all about us.
- Waiting brings a greater dependency on God. We have the opportunity to stop trying to do things our way.
- In waiting we find rest. Praying full of worry can end.
- Breakthrough is on the other side of the wait. We cannot give up.
- Waiting can draw us closer or drive us further from God. Choose wisely.
- Waiting reveals our hearts' attitudes. Adjust your heart appropriately.

How to find beauty in the wait:

- Stay thankful. Do not grumble and complain. (1 Thessalonians 5:18)
- Worship God. He is always worthy. (Psalm 42:11)
- Speak truth. Life and death are in the power of the tongue. (Proverbs 18:21)
- Expect God to be true to His character. He can be nothing but faithful. (Numbers 23:19)
- Take every thought captive. Do not agree with the devil's lies and accusations. (2 Corinthians 10:5)
- Wait on God as a waiter waits on those he is serving. Serve God and others. (Romans 12:10–11)
- Pray. Do not worry. (Philippians 4:6–7)
- Strengthen your faith. Do not waver in unbelief. (Romans 4:20)
- Hold tight to God's promises. Be fully convinced He is faithful to accomplish all He has promised. (Romans 4:21)

Waiting is not necessarily a trial, but it does test our faith in God and weighs our dependency on Jesus. Our main objective in waiting and in any other situation in life should be to know Him more. A lot of the time we get so focused on the fulfillment of a promise, it becomes our idol and we overlook the main thing: our relationship with Jesus.

We cannot forget Matthew 6:33, where we are instructed to seek God and His righteousness first, believing that as we do, He promises to provide all we need. In waiting, it is easy to seek the promise. And I understand how comforting it is to seek the promise, but that will not bring its fulfillment. We must believe, expect, and trust God for the promise, all the while seeking Jesus first.

I challenge you in your next waiting season not to waste the wait by getting distracted with fear and worry. Please allow God to forge His beauty in your heart and soul, the beauty of trusting Jesus that can be found in seasons of waiting.

It would greatly benefit you to stop and examine your faith. If there are areas that need solidifying, please take steps to heart hydration by strengthening your faith.

7

A HEART-STYLE OF THANKSGIVING

Thankfulness is vital to heart hydration. Thankfulness hydrates because it is the will of God. First Thessalonians 5:18 tells us, "In everything give thanks; for this is the will of God in Christ Jesus for you" (NKJV).

Why is thankfulness His will? God wants us to live a life of gratitude because He knows and understands what thankfulness accomplishes in our hearts, souls, and lives. A huge accomplishment of thankfulness is the ability to help us take our eyes off of our circumstances, causing us to refocus, to look higher than what we can see or touch, and to press beyond what our hearts and souls can feel.

Thankfulness also causes our hearts and souls to stay humble. In giving thanks for everything, we are reminded of one very simple but deep truth: what do we have that God has not given us? And if everything we possess and all we have achieved is a gift from God, how could we boast or take credit for it (1 Corinthians 4:7)?

HEART-STYLE

I love the Thanksgiving holiday. I love having all my kids in one place at one time! One of my favorite traditions takes place after our meal. We go around the table from person to person, and as we do, each one of us reflects on the past year and expresses what and whom each is thankful for. God, in His immeasurable goodness, takes thanksgiving to the highest level. It is not about a meal—it is about thousands of meals. It is not about gathering yearly but gathering daily. This should never happen just once a year following an abundant meal. A hydrated life lived in relationship with God is about having a thankful heart daily, in good times and in bad.

Essentially, thanksgiving is not just a lifestyle but a heart-style. This means we need to live this way as an automatic reflex where our hearts are conditioned to turn toward God, giving thanks for every situation in life. And because it is a heart-style, we cannot just meaninglessly murmur words of thanks. It is a heart issue, and it will require a change of heart. As you continue to read about the heart-hydrating benefits of thankfulness, determine to step into a heart-style of thanksgiving.

GIVE THANKS FOR *ALL* THINGS?

At first, I was shocked to find out that God wants us to give thanks for *all* things. *Really, all things?* Yes, all things as clearly stated in Ephesians 5:20: "Giving thanks always for all things to God the Father in the name of our Lord Jesus Christ" (NKJV). God is so radical!

My thoughts were, *How can it be God's will for me to give thanks for my child's rebellion?* At first, I resisted the concept because it did not seem logical—again, God's Word trumps man's logic. I am so thankful for Jesus' relentless mercy and grace.

One summer a few years back, I visited my dear friend, Teresa Elling. As usual, we talked nonstop, catching up on each other's lives. I began to explain my recent encounter with God where He had rearranged my heart and life by teaching me to give thanks for all things. I explained how two different random people had given me the same book to read, which seemed like an obvious nudging from God to read it. I excitedly told her about the phenomenon of giving thanks (as if it was a new idea).

Teresa interrupted me, asking, "What book?"

I told her it was *From Prison to Praise* by Merlin Carothers.

Looking surprised, she asked, "Do you remember when I talked to you about that book years ago?"

I was shocked to realize I had no memory of the conversation. Thoughts of regret were already swirling in my brain. *How could I not have remembered this? Is it because I had been so far removed from a thankful heart that I disregarded His promptings?*

Momentarily disliking myself, I asked her to tell me the story.

She reminded me of our visit years earlier. "You were telling me about your heartbreak over your son choosing not to follow God. I mentioned some Scriptures about giving thanks for everything and suggested that you try and thank God for where your son was at in life. I clearly recall your response."

I shuddered with embarrassment for my old ways of living in the Me factor. Silently I repented of my pride.

Teresa reluctantly went on, "You said, 'No, I will never.'"

Ugh. Way back then, God tried to give me the truth of His Word through that very same book. He wanted me to understand an essential component to life—the heart-style of thanksgiving. If only I had been humble and mature enough to receive it. Once again, I praised God for His tenacity, unrelenting love and mercy—thankful He was so patient with me.

Ironically, thirteen years later, I was facing yet again another one of my sons making the choice not to follow God, but this time I was able to face it with an entirely different perspective. Yes, I was grieved, but I knew because of Romans 8:28 that God turns all the messiness of life into something beautiful. Because of

God's faithfulness, I was able to thank Jesus for my son's life and his temporary season of wandering.

The heart hydration process has taught me to unswervingly trust God and His Word, to make Him enough for all situations. This has allowed me to trust my children into Jesus' hands, and I believe without a doubt His Word in Isaiah to be my children's reality: "For I will contend with him who contends with you, and I will save your children" (Isaiah 49:25b, NKJV). And also,

> I will pour out my Spirit on your offspring, and my bless-
> ing on your descendants. They will spring up like grass in
> a meadow, like poplar trees by flowing streams. Some
> will say, "I belong to the LORD"; others will call them-
> selves by the name of Jacob; still others will write on their
> hand, "The LORD's," and will take the name Israel. (Isaiah
> 44:3b–5, NIV)

NO ACCUSATION

The biggest revelation I have had about living a heart-style of thanksgiving is that thankfulness, especially in hard times, causes our hearts to stay soft toward Jesus. When we are thankful, there is no room to accuse or blame Him, a priceless aspect of thankful-ness, no doubt.

While in the learning stages of gratitude, my family experi-enced a season where all of our cars kept breaking down, one right after the other and most of the time in pairs. I had a large, very busy family, and everyone needed to be somewhere all the time. Our cars were at the point where they needed to be retired, not continually repaired. It was incredibly frustrating because this season lasted a long time—a really long time.

I faithfully prayed and asked for a newer car. Or did I faith-fully whine, moan, and complain to God about needing a newer car? Truthfully, it was the latter.

One day, it became clear by my grumbling I was accusing Jesus of not coming through for me. He showed me I needed to begin to thank Him for *not* having a working car. Thank Him for the season—thank Him for His grace in this season—thank Him for being good and faithful.

Thankfulness causes our hearts to be tender and trusting, full of faith instead of irritably wondering, *When will God come through for me?* and worse, *Why would He allow such suffering in my life?*

Gratitude is in essence putting on rose-colored glasses (the good kind). A heart-style of thanksgiving causes praise to abound in and through us, changing our perspective on life. It brings Philippians 4:11b–12 to life, "I have learned to be content whatever the circumstances. I know what it is to be in need, and I know what it is to have plenty. I have learned the secret of being content in any and every situation, whether well fed or hungry, whether living in plenty or in want" (NIV). Being content in any and every situation definitely means making Jesus enough!

PERSPECTIVE CHANGE

Stepping into living a heart-style of thanksgiving, where Jesus is enough, requires a change of perspective. In giving God thanks for all things, you will hydrate your heart because you will view Jesus and your life through the truth of His Word instead of through your own thoughts and feelings.

Once again, while on vacation at my friend Teresa's home in sunny California, I was sitting outside at a picnic table, blogging. I was facing their side yard to avoid distraction. When I looked up, I saw an empty dog run, dead grass, and a junk pile. From where I was sitting, that was my perspective. If I had sat there the whole three days and never moved or looked around, that would be all I would have seen and all I would have known of my friend's property. And when I returned home, all I would have had to say about Teresa's house was they did not have a dog, never watered their grass, and did not make dump runs.

I decided to make a shift. By simply turning, I saw a beautiful blue swimming pool with a welcoming diving board. Next to the pool was a pleasant outdoor, summer bed sitting under a spacious, covered patio where a bamboo ceiling fan slowly turned, cooling the air for the sleeping dog lying below. Painted and restored furniture held towels and pool toys. In addition, there was a barbeque and potted plants along the patio, and summer hats hung all in a row along the back wall. I spied fruit trees, green grass, a cute chicken coop, and a garden. From my new perspective, I was able to tell my family of all the beauty, creativity, and wonder of Teresa's inviting home.

Can you see the difference a change in perspective makes?

If you do not change your perspective and acquire a thankful heart, your heart will be dehydrated and apathetic. And you will view your life and God through the small lens of negativity, past experience, and complaint.

EVIDENCE

Living with a heart-style of thanksgiving is confirmation of true faith in God. In the previous chapter, we discussed unbelief and how it, not any problem we may have, is our biggest issue. Think about this for a moment: the opposite of a thankful heart is a grumbling and complaining heart. And a grumbling and complaining heart is a sure sign of an unbelieving heart.

I love the eleventh chapter of Hebrews—I call it the "by faith" chapter. When I read it, my faith is strengthened. The first verse reads, "Now faith is the substance of things hoped for, the evidence of things not seen" (NKJV). Being thankful is the evidence of things we cannot yet see, but by faith we believe them to be true.

The way it works is we live a faith-filled life by believing God's Word and applying it to every situation and circumstance. The next step after applying the Word is thankfulness. It is our evidence or assurance that He will do what He promises. Stepping into this heart-style will not only satisfy a thirsty heart, but it will set an assurance of His faithfulness in our hearts.

Here are some very practical ways to transition your heart and life into a heart-style of thanksgiving. Follow these simple steps until thankfulness becomes your automatic response.

- Ask for a change of heart in regard to being thankful.
- Daily make a list of all the things (good and bad) you are thankful for.
- Each time you pray, immediately thank Jesus for the answer.

Do not hesitate. Step into a thankful heart-style today!

Thirty-Day Challenge: For thirty days straight, do these three steps. At the end of the thirty days, assess your progress and take note of how your heart has changed.

8
LOVE AND OBEDIENCE

Learning to walk in the fear of the Lord deeply affects heart hydration. This one truth is capable of revolutionizing our lives merely because it helps clear out our hearts' clutter to focus on the essentials of living for God. The fear of the Lord helps us to grasp the tender love of God, causing our hearts to find peace and rest in obedience.

When the Lord first approached me on this subject, I was unmistakably baffled. *Fear the God of love? Why would God want us to be afraid of Him?* Relax—it is not that kind of fear. In this context, the definition for fear is reverence, awe, respect, and honor toward God.

My search for a deeper understanding of the fear of the Lord has unfolded this truth: friendship and intimacy with Him are reserved for those who fear Him. Psalm 25:14 says, "The Lord is a friend to those who fear him. He teaches them his covenant" (NLT). *The Message* says it like this: "God-friendship is for God-worshipers; they are the ones he confides in." If we want to live in close relationship with Jesus, it is important to learn the fear of the Lord.

OUR ALL

The capacity in which we are required to love Jesus necessitates the fear of the Lord. This is because of the way the Bible unapologetically tells us how much we are to love Him. Deuteronomy 10:12 says, "And now, Israel, what does the LORD your God require of you, but to fear the LORD your God, to walk in all His ways and to love Him, to serve the LORD your God with all your heart and with all your soul" (NKJV). And in Mark 12:30: And you shall love the LORD your God with all your heart, with all your soul, with all your mind, and with all your strength. This is the first commandment" (NKJV). Loving God with all our heart, soul, mind, and strength is an audacious, sometimes seemingly out-of-reach, way to live. How can mere people with such a human condition love in such a huge capacity? The real answer to that question is *we can't*. It is impossible unless we allow Him to pour His love in and through us. Knowing and operating in the fear of the Lord will assist us in loving Him the way He deserves. In reading this chapter, please keep the words of Deuteronomy 10:12 and Mark 12:30 in mind, and take note of how each aspect of the fear of the Lord empowers us to love him with our *all*.

The fear of the Lord is not an outdated concept, something only believed in biblical times. Since God is the same yesterday, today, and forever (Hebrews 13:8), there are no fads for biblical truths.

Why does God require us to fear Him and love Him with our all? Before I learned the fear of the Lord, I used to feel a little ticked off that Jesus wants all of me. Thankfully, He has changed my prideful heart and given me insight on the reason why He requires all, which is different from what the Me factor and the devil would make it out to be.

It is not because God is selfish but because He is jealous (Exodus 34:14). Our all-knowing God is jealous in the best way.

He loves us too much to let us give ourselves to meaningless, harmful lovers such as selfishness, brokenness, fear, pride, and confusion with our identity in Christ. He is a good Father and seeks the best for His children. His best for us is that we love Him with a faithful undivided heart, because this, to say the least, is where our hearts soar.

PRICELESS TREASURE

The fear of the Lord helps to unlock the ultimate treasure—a deeper, more intimate relationship with Jesus that encompasses friendship and intimacy, in essence not just knowing about Him but actually knowing Him personally. The word *know* is a Jewish expression for physical intimacy between a husband and wife. This reveals an aspect of closeness that can be found in emotional and spiritual intimacy with God. Since the church is defined as the bride of Christ, intimacy is the bride's privilege.

God is a friend to those who fear Him and He teaches them His covenant. A covenant seals the relationship between groom and bride; hence, our friendship with the Lord is one of intimacy. The Scripture makes it clear that this caliber of relationship is reserved for those who fear Him.

First Samuel 2:12 describes the sons of Eli as corrupt, saying they did not know God. Practically speaking, they did not fear Him. The sons of Eli were priests, and it was their job to minister to God, just as it is our job. They performed many rituals, going through all the motions but missing the main point. Let it not be said of us that we do not know God. Let us learn the fear of the Lord so all we do for Him will not be empty works, rituals, rules, or sacrifices.

The fear of the Lord etched on our hearts and souls helps us to enter into a love relationship where intimacy with God is found.

If you want to hear His voice better, know and do His will more, and if you desire heart hydration—*God's presence is your answer.* His presence is where every need is met.

WHAT?

What exactly is the fear of the Lord? The fear of the Lord is described as many things:

- "true wisdom" (Job 28:28, NLT)
- "clean [pure] enduring forever" (Psalm 19:9, NKJV)
- "the foundation of true knowledge" (Proverbs 1:7, NLT)
- "a fountain of life" (Proverbs 14:27, NKJV)
- "His treasure" (Isaiah 33:6, NKJV)
- "to hate evil" (Proverbs 8:13, NKJV)
- "healing" (Proverbs 3:7–8, NLT)

Consider the fear of the Lord as a gateway leading to many avenues of blessing. According to the Scriptures listed, we see that the fear of the Lord is the *key* to the passageway of wisdom, purity, knowledge, life, treasure, and good health.

WHY?

Why is the fear of the Lord a gateway or passageway to blessing, wisdom, and knowledge? Psalm 89:7 says, "God is greatly to be feared in the assembly of the saints, and to be held in reverence by all those around Him" (NKJV). Fearing God causes us to put Him in His rightful place and to see Him for who He truly is—God, Lord, and Master. He is not ordinary, average, or on the same level as we are but highly exalted, honored, respected, and obeyed. God acknowledges a reverent and obedient heart (Malachi 3:16–18). This is one reason the fear of the Lord is a gateway to an abundant life.

Understanding the fear of the Lord is one of those subjects that the Me factor is opposed to. Proverbs 2:3–5 gives us huge insight into comprehending the fear of the Lord. "Yes, if you cry out for discernment, and lift up your voice for understanding, if you seek her as silver, and search for her as for hidden treasures; then you will understand the fear of the LORD, and find the knowledge of God" (NKJV). If you cannot wrap your head around this truth, fervently search in the same way you would for silver or hidden treasure. Ask God for discernment and understanding of the fear of the Lord.

THE FEAR OF THE LORD EQUALS LOVE AND OBEDIENCE

Jesus is the treasure of heaven. I have learned that the easiest way to partake of the many jewels available in this treasure is best done when I willingly embrace obedience. I am not talking about living a legalistic life of rules but instead a life of grace and freedom. This is an obedient life that joyfully celebrates the ways of God with its actions.

In John 15:14, Jesus stated, "You are My friends if you do whatever I command you" (NKJV). First John 5:3 says, "Loving God means keeping his commandments, and his commandments are not burdensome" (NLT). Plainly, according to God's Word, we see love and obedience go hand in hand. I love how John 5:3 says His commandments are not burdensome. Loving God by obeying Him is not laborious or out of reach for a submitted heart and soul. God requiring obedience is a sign of His generous love. He cares enough for us; therefore, he calls us to obedience. Parents do not make their children obey because they are mean. They require obedience because they love them and know what is best for their precious children.

Please realize obedience is a required benefit, not a choice. And there are no gray areas when it comes to obedience, only black and white, implying there is no middle road, no casual, selective, or fractional obedience. Obedience is a heart issue. If you have difficulty with obedience, ask God to change your heart. Psalm 55:19b tells us, "Because they do not change, therefore they do not fear God" (NKJV).

When we operate in the understanding of the fear of the Lord, we will operate in obedience, therefore operating in love. After many years of living in partial obedience, doing as I pleased, I realized my heart and life were parched partly because I was not schooled in the fear of the Lord. Your heart may remain dehydrated until you get into rhythm with this reality.

In 1 Samuel 15, we find the account of King Saul. Verses 2 and 3 inform us the Lord instructed Saul to go to battle: "This is what the LORD of Heaven's Armies has declared: 'I have decided to settle accounts with the nation of Amalek for opposing Israel when they came from Egypt. Now go and completely destroy the entire Amalekite nation—men, women, children, babies, cattle, sheep, goats, camels, and donkeys'" (NLT). Verses 7–9 explain that Saul slaughtered the Amalekites and spared Agag, the Amalekite king. He kept the best of the sheep and goats, the cattle, the fat calves, the lambs, and everything that appealed to them. They destroyed only what was worthless.

Now wait a minute. Didn't the Lord tell Saul to completely destroy *all?*

In verse 11, the Lord said to Samuel the prophet, "I am sorry that I ever made Saul king, for he has not been loyal to me and has refused to obey my command" (NLT). Saul grieved the Lord to the point that He was sorry He ever appointed him as king.

In verse 20, we read Saul's response to Samuel's accusation that Saul did not obey God: "'But I did obey the LORD,' Saul insisted. 'I carried out the mission he gave me. I brought back King Agag, but I destroyed everyone else. Then my troops brought in the best of the sheep, goats, cattle, and plunder to sacrifice to the LORD your God in Gilgal'" (NLT).

Saul used sacrifice to cover up his fractional obedience. Saul did *almost* all that God asked of Him, and yet, he grieved the heart of God.

Samuel replied to Saul in verse 22, "What is more pleasing to the Lord: your burnt offerings and sacrifices or your obedience to his voice? Listen! Obedience is better than sacrifice, and submission [the "s" word again] is better than offering the fat of rams" (NLT). Saul's reason for disobeying God is found in verse 24. "Then Saul admitted to Samuel, 'Yes, I have sinned. I have disobeyed your instructions and the Lord's command [will], for I was afraid of the people and did what they demanded'" (NLT). Saul failed to yield to and follow God's will. His heart was divided and self-centered, and he cared more for his own desires; consequently, he catered to the fear, approval, and acceptance of people, rather than God.

THE FEAR OF MAN VERSUS THE FEAR OF THE LORD

The fear of man can be described as needing man's approval more that God's approval, caring more about what people think of us than what God thinks of us. Proverbs 29:25 gives us insight: "The fear of man brings a snare, but whoever trusts in the Lord shall be safe" (NKJV). A sobering fact is that God's opinion of us should be the *only* one of real importance.

Matthew 10:28 frankly states, "And do not fear those who kill the body but cannot kill the soul. But rather fear Him who is able to destroy both soul and body in hell" (NKJV). Why would we waste our lives fearing men who can only affect our human bodies? Rather, fear God, the only one who can destroy both body and soul for eternity. The fear of the Lord causes us to be aware of who we are in Him, instead of striving to be someone who lives to please people or culture. Abandoning the Me factor with all of its selfish and prideful desires makes it much easier to step out of living a life dictated by the opinion of others.

The fear of the Lord can be summed up in two words: love and obedience. Please remember the fear of the Lord is not just something we gain knowledge of but is to become a part of who we are. The fear of the Lord *in* us causes our hearts and souls to be mindful of Him. It will cause us to discontinue a casual attitude of treating God and His Word as commonplace, therefore causing heart hydration.

Use this moment to ask God to give you greater understanding and to engrave the biblical principle of the fear of the Lord on your heart.

9

HEALING THE HEART AND SOUL

Let's face it. Life is messy—really messy. And in this messiness, people get hurt. The heart, soul, and especially the emotions of most people are in need of healing in some form or another. Some people need to be healed from incidents that happened in childhood, others from various life situations that have left a wound, imprinting their heart and soul—dictating the way they love and live.

Two of my favorite attributes of Jesus are that He is the Healer and the Deliverer. His love heals a broken heart and delivers a suffering soul. He is not a God who demands from His people. No, He is a giver; He extends tender mercy in the form of healing love and abundant grace. Please know you do not have to work for this incredible gift of healing. You only need to surrender to it.

I have talked a lot about how Jesus has hydrated my heart and life through healing. In this chapter I will give you a closer look into my healing process, providing key components that can hydrate your heart and soul to help you step into the healing the cross has already provided for you. I pray that my experiences will help you step into heart hydration at the deepest level. Please do not get nervous—you are ready to go deeper!

HEALING THE INSIDE

As you know by now, my life, to say the least, was messy. You also know that faithful Jesus has healed me of this messiness. My heart and soul were wounded and broken from unfaithfulness, betrayal, and death. The healing I received regarding these intruders is priceless. When I first became a believer, I did not understand what the whole package of Christianity entailed. In time I learned that Jesus was much more than my Savior and prayer-answer man. As I began to trust Him, I found Him to be the only one who cares deeply about every aspect of my life. His sacrifice on the cross made a way for me to be healed and delivered from the wounds life left on my heart and soul.

When a person gets hurt, the wound leaves the heart and soul empty, impaired, and damaged. A natural, common reaction to being wounded and brokenhearted is to aimlessly fill the emptiness and cover up the damage. This is a crucial time—what a person does at this point matters tremendously. The best and quickest way to get through the pain is to immediately turn to Jesus and step into His healing, recognizing He has already made a way for us on the cross and He is enough.

But unfortunately, instead of giving our broken hearts and pain over to Jesus, in our weakness and confusion, we sometimes unconsciously let substitutes fill the emptiness of our hearts and souls. These intruders can be lies, blame-shifting, unforgiveness, self-protection, mistrust, unbelief, depression, workaholism, shame, guilt, fear of man, performance-based relationships, antidepressants, therapists, compulsive behaviors, rebellion, anger, revenge, satanism, the occult, fear, and control.

Other substitutes and intruders are addictions. Addictions to self (the Me factor), alcohol, food, drugs, sex, pornography, lying, selfishness, the opposite sex, social media, and gossip attempt to fill the emptiness inside. Worse, when wounded we can withdraw completely from God, the very One who can help us. When we unknowingly try to use these things as a substitute for Him, we will continue in our woundedness and live with a dehydrated heart and soul.

Psalm 147:3 says, "He heals the brokenhearted and binds up their wounds" (NKJV). This is our promise. At the cross, we trade a wounded heart and soul for His healing and wholeness. Some people struggle for years on end with a dehydrated heart and soul, battling with the same issues over and over. They are seemingly incapable of getting free, even though they have tried for years.

Although there is a myriad of reasons why this happens, here are just three.

1. *Unbelief.* Struggle is prolonged first through unbelief in God's love—unbelief that the cross has already paid for all sin and brokenness, and second, unbelief in God's goodness and willingness to help. This happens primarily because His goodness is measured and judged by the amount of suffering that is allowed in an individual or in the world. Also, negative experiences can lead to blaming God and not trusting His love. I used to believe that God could help me, but I was not sure He would. Jesus with His healing love taught my heart how to trust Him. Now I live my life from the stance of believing God is able and willing to help me.

    Unbelief cannot be permitted to exist in the heart of a believer; it is a snare that has to be ruthlessly dealt with. If not, the enemy will effortlessly continue to entrap the believer. Psalm 106:24 states, "The people refused to enter the pleasant land, for they wouldn't believe his promise to care for them" (NLT). Unbelief will debilitate people and consequently not allow them to enter into God's promise of rest (healing). Believers must be convinced of God's faithfulness to them personally.

2. *Wounds*: Some people have been deeply and consistently hurt and are so full of pain stuffed so deeply that they do not recognize its presence or realize how it dictates their behavior. Sometimes this is evident in a person's life by the inability to love or be loved, a resistance to enter into close relationships, inability to make Jesus enough, the presence of sin or addictions, or a cycle of continual bad choices.

3. *Selfishness*: When people get hurt, betrayed, or abused, especially in childhood, they learn to self-protect, which leads to a lifestyle of selfishness filled with self-sufficiency. When people live in self-will, they become blinded by being their own god, leaving no room for Jesus. This ultimately leads to more pain, not only to the person but to those the person has relationships with, especially on an intimate level.

As for those of us who have deep issues, we will not be able to walk in victory unless we let Jesus into our hearts and lives. Some people think letting Him in will cause more pain and are afraid of the healing process. This is a lie that the devil uses to keep people in bondage. Staying strong in your faith in Jesus and His accomplishment on the cross will help keep you free. Do not listen to the devil's lies.

For most, being wounded leads to numbness. I know because I have experienced this very thing, and you may recognize it in your life. It is as if you are paralyzed. Although you can see the road of freedom you should be traveling on, you are incapable of getting to the road. Why? Because you have depleted all of your energy—you are spent. Your strength has been used facilitating and covering up your pain and emptiness. This is how casual, fake, or performance-based Christianity is achieved.

If you can identify with this, then you are right where you should be. You must realize you cannot help yourself; you have nothing left, and your strength is gone. Most times, you have to come completely to the end of yourself to finally let God take over.

This takes humility. I know because I have had to humble myself many times (and I am positive I will have to in the future). Jesus loves and embraces the humble, but He resists the proud (this does not mean He does not love the proud). I have never liked the idea of being resisted by Him. How about you? When we try to get better on our own, we are displaying independence and pride. We have to realize that all of our efforts outside of Christ are pointless works that only lead to more selfish living.

Another area that keeps wounded people from freedom is blame shifting. We must own our issues and stop shifting the blame onto others. People may have hurt us, but the past really is the past, and we are responsible for the here and now. If we do not take this responsibility seriously, heart hydration will be delayed.

You have a treasure in Jesus—He is for you. He always has your back. And because of this, He will never call you to an impossible task but will always equip you to succeed in whatever He asks of you.

Healing and deliverance may seem like impossible tasks, but they are actually keys to freedom. They should be viewed as the tenderness of God, His mercy, grace, and goodness, that will unlock a thriving relationship with Jesus, bringing a flood of hydration to a thirsty heart and soul.

These key components have helped me heal and keep me hydrated:
- Knowing the Holy Spirit
- Truly repenting
- Being forgiven and extending forgiveness

- Receiving deliverance
- Severing unhealthy connections
- Recognizing and healing the root cause
- Inviting Jesus into wounded places
- Knowing how to stay free
- Knowing how to deal with new offenses

The most valuable component to my healing process is not on the list—these are the mechanics of healing. What healed and changed me the most was falling in love with God the Father and Jesus. Getting to know God's gentle, kind, tender, and compassionate love is what melted the hardness of my heart and healed the depths of who I am. This love crumbled the walls around my heart, hydrating me inside and out.

As you read about these essential components to stepping into healing, ask Jesus to help you understand and apply each one as needed. Also, I ask that you will please seek to draw nearer to Jesus. I would hate for you to go through all the motions of healing and not engage with the Healer Himself—He is the essence of heart hydration.

THE HOLY SPIRIT

Without the direction and power of the Holy Spirit, we are left to know God in the strength and wisdom of our natural minds, and we all know how that goes. When we submit to letting the Holy Spirit direct our lives, our human condition is put in its rightful place. Galatians 5:16 says, "So I say, let the Holy Spirit guide your lives. Then you won't be doing what your sinful nature craves" (NLT). It is also important to realize God is Spirit, and we are to worship Him in spirit and truth (John 4:24). The spirit is His Holy Spirit, and the truth is His Word. When Jesus died and went to heaven, Father God sent us the Holy Spirit (John 14:26), our gift and power here on earth. Shying away from the Holy Spirit does not make sense because He is our Helper.

A friend of mine used to see a therapist for help in dealing with depression. What amazed me about the situation was the therapist seemed powerless. He could talk about the problems causing depression and take this person back to the point of pain, hoping to acquire a different perspective of the hurtful incident. That was it: "Here is your prescription. See you next week." The power of the Holy Spirit and the loving presence of Jesus were absent to deeply heal and change my friend.

Every believer should have a relationship with the Holy Spirit. In doing so, we are identified as belonging to God:

> And when you believed in Christ, he identified you as his own by giving you the Holy Spirit, whom he promised long ago. The Spirit is God's guarantee that he will give us the inheritance he promised and that he has purchased us to be his own people. He did this so we would praise and glorify him. (Ephesians 1:13b–15, NLT)

Are you missing out on the complete relationship you should be having with God?

TRUE REPENTANCE

Does the word repentance make you a little uneasy? I hope not, because it is very beneficial to heart hydration. Repentance is often difficult but only because of pride. I love what Isaiah says about God and the repentant person: "I live in the high and holy place with those whose spirits are contrite and humble. I restore the crushed spirit of the humble and revive the courage of those with repentant hearts" (Isaiah 57:15, NLT). Read that again. He revives the courage of those who have repentant hearts. If your heart is dehydrated by the cruelty of life, you need courage to continue living and to keep your heart soft and hydrated.

Repentance is a lethal weapon in the hand of the believer. Not that we grovel before God every day, never feeling worthy or forgiven. Rather, we simply realize in our human condition we are prone to human behavior, such as selfishness—which most of the time needs repentance! And we must also realize that Christians can get stuck in bondage to sin. It would be foolishness to think we repent only once when we first decide to live for God. The cross has paid for all sin past, present, and future, but that does not give us license to treat the grace of God casually or with disrespect (Romans 6:1).

Without repentance, our flesh remains prideful. It is what we do with our sin that makes all the difference. If we hide our sin and defend ourselves, making excuses for our behavior, we can stray far from God. The distance is not because He is mad at us or does not love us but because we are honoring sin, allowing it to rule our hearts and souls, rather than the power of the cross.

To obtain freedom from sin, whether it be unintentional, hidden, or otherwise, it needs to be confessed *and* repented. We first need to confess to God. Second, it might be necessary to also confess to someone we can trust (preferably someone who will give us good, solid advice). Third, we more than likely will also need to confess to those we have sinned against (Matthew 5:23–24; James 5:16). When my husband was in the thick of his sin, he knew he needed to repent and confess his sin not only to God, but to me, and to someone who could help him step out of his sin. For years he wrestled with this and would only confess to God. This caused him to lack accountability or good counsel and to keep his sin hidden.

Confession uncovers sin, taking it out of the darkness and bringing it into the light. It loosens us from sin's grip, therefore removing its heavy burden off of our hearts, souls, and lives. (Please note: it really is better you expose your own sin rather than waiting until you are caught.)

The act of repentance is simple. We turn to merciful Jesus and, without reservation, confess our sin and say we are sorry for sinning against Him and whoever else might be involved. Then we ask for His forgiveness and grace and ask Him to fill us with His love and faithfulness. In repentance, we are not just acknowledging, confessing, and apologizing for our sin, but seeking a change of heart and soul. Our mind must be renewed about our sin so that we can turn from it (Romans 12:1–2).

Acts 3:19 says, "Repent, then, and turn to God, so that your sins may be wiped out, that times of refreshing may come from the Lord" (NIV). When our heart is changed, our mind renewed, and we turn from our sin, our life will not only be refreshed, but it will produce fruit of righteousness (Hebrews 12:11). Our palate for sin changes, and sin becomes distasteful.

Sincerity about sin not only leads us to freedom but to godly sorrow, which opens the door to true repentance. Godly sorrow is the grief we experience when we realize we have sinned against God Himself. Read what 2 Corinthians 7:10 says regarding true repentance and godly sorrow: "For the kind of sorrow God wants us to experience leads us away from sin and results in salvation. There's no regret for that kind of sorrow. But worldly sorrow, which lacks repentance, results in spiritual death" (NLT).

The sorrow the world has to offer leads to death because it has nothing to do with *true* repentance; therefore, no changes are made. Worldly sorrow cheaply spits the words "I'm sorry" out of its mouth, desperately trying to relieve its own conscience. It is all about self with no real regard for God or those it has hurt and wounded, which is why it leads to death—as selfishness always does. Casual Christians treat repentance as if it were the cold ocean where they just tiptoe along the shore. Since we sincerely want heart hydration and a deeper relationship with God, then we cannot afford to be casual.

We also have to remember how tenderhearted and patient Jesus is, knowing He is not out to hit us over the head with the weight of our sin, but His purposes are to lift our burden and draw us nearer to Him. Romans 2:4 says, "Don't you see how wonderfully kind, tolerant, and patient God is with you? Does this mean nothing to you? Can't you see that His kindness is intended to turn you from your sin?" (NLT).

Finally, when we confess, repent, and ask for forgiveness, Jesus takes our sin and remembers it no more. He removes our sin as far from us as the east is from the west (Psalm 103:12). Please do not keep reminding yourself and Him of it by continually repenting of the same sin and feeling weighed down by guilt and shame. Simply shut the mouth of the devil and be led by the Holy Spirit. Remember Romans 8:1: "There is therefore now no condemnation to those who are in Christ Jesus, who do not walk according to the flesh, but according to the Spirit" (NKJV). When we live in the Spirit and not the flesh, there is no condemnation or shame. Oh, thank God for that!

One way to know if we are operating in true repentance is to check our condemnation level. True repentance sets us free with no regret. The enemy of our soul will try to convince us we are not forgiven, healed, or delivered. He will attempt to heap shame on us, but we have to remember: *if we sincerely repent and operate in godly sorrow, God forgives us.* End of story. If living in the freedom of forgiveness is difficult for you, you just might need to forgive yourself. Forgiving yourself is essentially the same as accepting God's forgiveness. Do not be so hard on yourself. You may have made a mess of things, but if God forgives you, then who are you not to forgive yourself?

THE "F" WORD—FORGIVE

To enjoy the benefits of true repentance and to step into heart hydration, we need to come face to face with the truth about forgiveness.

The one thing I know about forgiveness is it is double-sided. The side we adore is the one I just mentioned—when I repent, God forgives me—I have a fresh slate. Yippee!

The other side of forgiveness is we must forgive others, no matter what they have done. In fact, God will not forgive us *unless* we forgive others. Mark 11:26 expresses this truth. In this passage, Jesus said, "But if you do not forgive, neither will your Father in heaven forgive your trespasses" (NKJV). In *The Message*, it is stated this way: "If you have anything against someone, forgive—only then will your heavenly Father be inclined to also wipe your slate clean of sins." This can pose a problem for someone who has a difficult time forgiving.

As a child, I grew up in a home where forgiveness was not a theme we lived by. Actually, I knew nothing about the subject—it was not even in my vocabulary! Oh, but God in His faithfulness has taught me the freedom of painstaking forgiveness. I am not going to sugarcoat this. Forgiving someone who has hurt, betrayed, or offended you is not easy—that is why I call it the "f" word!

Forgiving is hard because most times it's personal. It is easier to forgive someone who has not sinned directly against us, but forgiving a person who has hurt, betrayed, lied, or broken our hearts and lives personally, intentionally or not, is very difficult. And usually it is not a one-time decision. As we work through forgiving, we might have to forgive over and over again until the work of forgiveness is complete in our hearts.

The foremost aspect to remember about forgiveness is genuine forgiveness comes from a heart of gratitude that has experienced forgiveness. We forgive out of the abundance of forgiveness we ourselves have received from our merciful God.

One might think, *I haven't done anything to need forgiveness.* But according to the Bible, we are all born sinners needing the Savior and His forgiveness (Romans 5:18–19). On the cross, Jesus pardoned our sin, making it possible for us to pardon the sin of those who sin against us. If you have yet to ask Jesus to forgive you and to be Lord of your life, I invite you to do so. By now I hope you understand the tender, faithful love of God. Please do not delay. Trust me; everyone needs the Savior. Say a prayer right now—you will never regret it!

My friend Wilma Dee explained how to forgive in this manner: "Ask God to pour His forgiveness in through you and then out to those you need to forgive." What I like about Wilma's words of wisdom is that they explain how it is *God's* forgiveness, not ours, that does the work. What a relief! I do not have it in me—no matter how much Scripture I quote or how many times I speak it aloud—to thoroughly forgive. But when it is Jesus' forgiveness doing the work in and through us, we can be at peace. We can rest because our confidence is no longer in our efforts. All we have to do is choose to forgive.

Before I learned how to thoroughly forgive, I struggled because I knew I wanted to forgive, but deep in my heart where the pain was, I simply chose not to. There is some strange falsehood that says if we withhold forgiveness, we will be justified and the person needing the forgiveness will suffer. The truth is choosing not to forgive is like purposely ingesting poison, then waiting for the *other* person to die. The only problem is it will kill us, and often the other person remains unaffected. Our hearts will remain dehydrated and immature unless we choose to receive, step into, and extend forgiveness.

LIBERATE

A lot of people get turned off from the term deliverance, thinking it is some weird sort of religious practice. It is only as weird as you make it. Deliverance simply means salvation and the act of liberating. Psalm 18:2 says this about Jesus: "The LORD is my rock, my fortress and my deliverer; my God is my rock, in whom I take refuge, my shield and the horn of my salvation, my stronghold" (NIV). Nothing weird about it, just the fact—Jesus is our Deliverer. We should be very happy about this, because more than likely, we all need deliverance or breakthrough in some form or another.

Deliverance is doing the same work Jesus did. The Spirit of the Lord was on Him, and He was anointed to bring deliverance to the captives (Luke 4:18); likewise, the Spirit of the Lord and deliverance are available to us. The liberating act of deliverance brings a flood of heart hydration. Mainly because it takes (delivers) us out of and away from the things that interfere with having an intimate relationship with Jesus. It removes the clutter we talked about earlier and frees us from negative influences.

A lot of believers spend the majority of their lives repeating the same behaviors and mistakes, never really experiencing breakthrough. Unfortunately, this was true for my husband and me. I've appropriately heard this cycle called the Christian cul-de-sac. My interpretation of this is that day after day, year after year, and sadly, decade after decade, we keep going in circles, never making choices to change our hearts and lives. Instead, we accept ourselves the way we are and call it "good enough." This form of existence can cause us to live small, purposeless, unhealed, unfruitful lives, which is in direct opposition to who we are in Christ.

The power of the cross has definitely bought freedom for every believer. Going through a deliverance procedure is not necessarily required, but unfortunately, some get caught in unbelief and sin and do not know how to escape the devil's influence, therefore finding it difficult to step into that freedom. Healing, deliverance prayers, and severing unhealthy connections are vital tools that can be used to loosen us from the Christian cul-de-sac, as well as the devil's influences.

When I was first introduced to deliverance, way back in the early nineties, it was as if I had struck gold! I had been a believer for about fourteen years, but I had lived in a lot of bondage to sin. I did not understand that the freedom of the cross was mine if I would only believe. Consequently, I suffered because of the many strongholds in my life. Of course, I was not aware of the cause and thought, *That's just who I am.*

The freedom I received after deliverance changed my life, but it caused me to be a bit out of focus. I started to think deliverance was the answer to everything. However, ten years after my husband went through deliverance and was still struggling with the same stronghold issues, I realized deliverance was not the answer. Jesus is the answer, and deliverance is just the tool. (The tool of deliverance that I am specifically talking about is a deliverance prayer. It is when you or someone else intentionally prays for freedom from specific strongholds. This may sound complicated or scary, but it's not.)

Over time, I also understood we could have walked in freedom from the very beginning of our Christian lives, with or without using a deliverance prayer. This is a fact for every believer. The cross is enough, but sometimes tools are needed to access it. These tools are not the source of freedom; they are just a means to the freedom provided by the cross. Remember, the purpose to all methods and tools used in this book is to turn the focus of our hearts to a relationship with Jesus, restoring our hearts to a vibrant, hydrated state.

When we get stuck in woundedness (hurt, brokenheartedness, pain) and sin, deliverance is a tool that can help free us to live in the victory Christ died to give us, therefore hydrating our hearts and souls at a very deep level. There is *not* one specific way God does this. I have received freedom from issues I struggled with in various ways, such as praying deliverance prayers or while in worship, where His presence simply washed me clean. I also have experienced liberty during my own prayer and Bible time or when hearing the Word preached. God is not limited to how He can work in our lives. Please do not get stuck on the methods of deliverance; just know it is Jesus' desire that you live in His provided freedom.

To better understand this kind of freedom, you need to understand strongholds. A stronghold is anything that has a strong grip on you. Psalm 18:2 says God is to be our stronghold. That is an example of a healthy stronghold; it is the unhealthy strongholds we want freedom from.

Strongholds may be issues a person has tried to get free from but seems powerless over. Many of the common strongholds that negatively influence us are unbelief, rebellion, pride, poverty, love of money, greed, oppression, independence from God, fear, bondage to sin, all forms of selfishness, infirmity, jealousy, lawlessness, control, rejection, abandonment, addictions, anger, rage, pity, suicide, deception, lying, seduction, perversion, adultery, fornication, and sexual immorality. Oftentimes the devil will take advantage of a wounded person, leading them by a lie, to fill their woundedness with anything but Jesus, causing a stronghold to grip them.

Strongholds can come from sin choices. Romans 6:16 shows us, "Don't you realize that you become the slave of whatever you choose to obey? You can be a slave to sin, which leads to death, or you can choose to obey God, which leads to righteous living" (NLT). When we choose to obey sin, we open the door for it, enabling it to strongly grip our hearts, souls, and lives. Strongholds can also come from unresolved woundedness and generational sins that are handed down to us by parents who have not dealt with their own sin and strongholds (Exodus 34:7).

We should not take strongholds lightly, but we also should not fear them. Second Corinthians 10:4 tells us, "For the weapons of our warfare are not carnal but mighty in God for pulling down strongholds" (NKJV). Jesus, our Deliverer, is our weapon of warfare. Since Jesus has already defeated strongholds, dealing with them is simple.

First, ask Him to reveal to you any strongholds you may have. Second, recognize your freedom as a provision of the cross and as your right as a believer. Recognize it as the mercy, grace, and love of God for you. Third, attend to root causes (more information on root causes to follow). Fourth, pray a prayer of deliverance.

In the following prayer, there are a few important components worth mentioning. Along with repentance and forgiveness is renouncing or voluntarily disowning the stronghold. Then, there is the concept of exchanging—making a trade. For example, if you are being delivered from a stronghold of fear, exchange it for faith. The next part is the best because it's the healing portion: invite Jesus to fill and heal your heart and soul at their depths.

This is a suggested prayer. You can pray this one or make up your own. It does not need to be a formal ritual, but it does need to be sincere. If you are not willing to live a submitted lifestyle, to let go of sin and unhealthy relationships, then you should probably wait to pray deliverance prayers until you are ready.

Jesus, I recognize _____ to be a stronghold in my life. I repent and ask forgiveness for allowing it to influence my life. In Jesus name I renounce _____. I break its power over my mind, will, and emotions, over my heart, spirit, and body, over my past and my future. I exchange the stronghold of _____ for _____.

I choose to forgive _____. Jesus, fill me with Your healing presence. Go deep into the root cause and heal this place with Your love, forgiveness, and acceptance. Thank You that because of Your sacrifice on the cross, I am free. Strengthen me and my faith to stand strong and remember who I am in You. Amen.

DETAILS

Some people are afraid to move forward because they do not think they can stop bad behavior. For sure, that is the devil's plan. God wants your willingness to love Him enough to want to change and live free, and by God's grace, you will be able to step into all He has for you. Deliverance feels like a cool refreshing wave washing over you. It can change your perspective and help you step into the provision of the cross.

What scares some people is the thought that strongholds are demonic. Well, yes, after all, we are dealing with the devil and with principalities. Ephesians 6:12 gives a clear picture of this: "For we do not wrestle against flesh and blood, but against principalities, against powers, against the rulers of the darkness of this age, against spiritual hosts of wickedness in the heavenly places" (NKJV). However, these are not to be feared. Remember, Jesus has already triumphed over Satan. Grasp the truth of this very powerful Scripture found in Colossians 2:15: "Having disarmed principalities and powers, He made a public spectacle of them, triumphing over them in it" (NKJV). You must believe and have faith in the work of the cross and resurrection of Jesus. Remember who you are. Because of the cross, you have authority over the devil. Believe that Jesus has disarmed evil, and choose to walk in your freedom.

UNHEALTHY CONNECTIONS

If we have reached for comfort, dependence, fulfillment, or wholeness from people or things other than Jesus, then we more than likely have created connections that dehydrate our hearts and damage our relationship with Jesus. Untangling ourselves from these connections is very hydrating to our hearts and souls, because in severing unhealthy connections, we are detaching ourselves from things that hinder our relationship with Jesus. We step into a deeper level with Jesus and allow Him to be all He desires to be in our hearts and souls.

Most unhealthy connections are made with people we have improperly associated with. Also we may have connected ourselves to controlling or manipulative people.

Sexual ties are very strong and usually the most influential. Sex not only knits the heart and soul together but causes you to become physically one with whomever you have sexual relations with. Unhealthy bonds can also form by an ungodly agreement, vow, or covenant. These can be established by pledging your love to someone you used to date with words similar to "I'll always love you" or "I'm forever yours." One sign of an unhealthy connection is if you randomly long for, fantasize, or dream about an ex-lover, bringing back old familiar feelings that are not necessarily healthy for you or for your current relationship.

In my life, I have personally broken unhealthy ties with sexual abusers, ex-lovers, boyfriends, friends, siblings, my spouse, my children, places, miscarried and aborted babies, parents, pastors, and deceased loved ones.

If you need help in dealing with unhealthy connections, prayerfully make a list of the people you need to disconnect from. After making your list, pray over each name on it.

The following is a simple prayer you can use—please do not haphazardly go through this prayer. Severing these connections will bring you freedom, but only if you plan on *not* reconnecting your tie. You have to choose to step into your freedom and to stay free. Of course, you can pray more as God leads; this is just a basic approach to sever unhealthy connections that are *not* sexual.

Please read the entirety of this chapter before praying. In the following chapter, sexual brokenness and unhealthy connections are discussed in detail. *Please read that chapter before breaking sexual ties.* For those of you who have ties to the occult, satanism, witchcraft, fortune telling, psychics, horoscopes, card reading, Ouija board, and so on, it is very important not to go through these steps by yourself. Ask a pastor or someone who is familiar with this kind of prayer to pray with you.

> Jesus, I repent and ask forgiveness for establishing and maintaining this connection. In Jesus' name, I sever this unhealthy connection with _____. I break it over my heart, my mind, will, and emotions, my spirit, and my body. I sever this tie over my memory, over my past, and over my future. Forgive me for allowing this relationship to influence me in an unhealthy way. I choose to forgive _____. I submit to You. Fill me with Your love. Amen.

The method of severing unhealthy connections and breaking strongholds should be used as needed. Whenever I am struggling with a relationship or with forgiving someone, God usually points me in this direction. After I break the tie with the person, my struggle ceases and I am free to listen to God and just love the person.

One example is this: One of my close family members disowned me, and when I read the e-mail informing me, I was crushed. Heartbroken, I sat in my chair, thinking of all the things

I could e-mail back, then I turned to Jesus and said, "I have got to find You in this. I cannot let this define me." Jesus revealed to me I was tied to this person in an improper way. It made perfect sense (light bulb). Immediately, I began praying and severing the unhealthy connection. Instantly, the weight lifted and my thoughts cleared, and I could sincerely respond with a simple "I love you." If I ever had a doubt about unhealthy ties being real or affecting my whole being, it was dispelled at that very moment. My newfound freedom was real and tangible.

HEALING THE ROOT CAUSE

The root cause of any issue is where the heart and soul need healing. Strongholds and unhealthy connections can be viewed as symptoms to the root cause—a much deeper issue. In my life, for example, my root causes were fatherlessness and sexual abuse. The strongholds of rejection, abandonment, fear, and disappointment stemmed from these. My biggest issues (not trusting God and men, building walls to protect my heart, maintaining control, and seeking approval from the opposite sex) also stemmed from my root causes.

It is important to recognize and deal with the root cause of the issue you are seeking deliverance, disconnection, and healing from. It is helpful to view a root cause as a deep, oozing cut or wound. If you do not clean and care for the wound but just cover it up, it will not heal properly. No matter how much you ignore it, the toxins will scar and shape your life. People who continually struggle with the same sin over and over probably have not dealt with the root cause of their brokenness.

Can you identify any root causes in your life related to strongholds or unhealthy connections?

Healing these wounds is very important. It may take a little more time for this healing process as compared to breaking strongholds and severing unhealthy connections. Make sure to give yourself time to heal.

Inviting Jesus into the place of the root cause is probably the most important step. This is where hydration is accessed at the deepest level. Through faith and by His grace, you are allowing Him into the core of who you are. Be assured: He is beyond faithful and will fill and heal all brokenheartedness, wounds, emptiness, and pain.

Allow Him to hydrate the depths of your heart and soul, to live in and be at home at the very core of who you are. In doing so, your heart will be full, leaving no room for root causes to remain and dictate your life.

Make sure to prayerfully deal with all root causes:

1. Ask Jesus to reveal any incidents or memories that wounded you.

2. Identify any strongholds or unhealthy connections related to those incidents or memories.

3. Recognize the root cause of any stronghold and unhealthy connection.

4. Invite Jesus into the root cause—give this tender place in your heart and soul over to Him.

5. Forgive any and all involved, and very importantly yourself.

6. Ask Jesus to fill and heal you at the core of your issue.

7. Believe that you are healed.

The last four steps might need to be done over and over until you can fully live in your healing. It is important to remember the truth that the cross bought your healing. Your faith in this truth will help you to step into it.

CONTEND FOR YOUR FREEDOM

The enemy of your soul is not content to just let you step into your destiny and relationship with Jesus—imagine that! He lives to rob you of your faith. If you are not going to live a submitted lifestyle and seek to be filled with Jesus after healing, deliverance, and severing unhealthy connections, you might end up in worse shape than before you started. Therefore, contend for your freedom.

Sometimes, bombardment of some sort will come after these types of healing prayers. This makes perfect sense, since the enemy of your soul hates you and will always try to steal your freedom. It is *extremely* important, especially right after deliverance, to stay in God's presence, seeking His filling. Being in His presence—the Word, worship, praise, thanksgiving, and prayer—is how we fill up and contend. You may also want to talk and pray with your pastor, a friend, or loved one who will support you through this healing adventure.

You cannot heal or deliver yourself; you are simply using tools *by faith in God* to help you step into freedom. God has not given you one fix-all tool to make you better. If He did, because of your human condition, you would stop looking for Him and search for the tool. Again, the main point I want to stress is all of this is for heart hydration leading to a deeper relationship with Jesus. You must be willing to, by grace, draw closer to Him.

Remember that if Christ sets you free, then you are free (John 8:36). The enemy will try to harass you. My advice is to stand firm. This simply means do not reopen the doors to old sin habits, not even a crack! Do not let your heart and soul wander from the truth that the cross has set you free. You are worthy of freedom, and most importantly, you are so valuable to God that He made a way for you.

HEALING THE HEART AND SOUL

If you find choosing to move forward difficult or if you struggle between the old habit of your sin and freedom, please do not beat yourself up, and certainly do not give up. I think this is where people lose the battle and give up on walking in the freedom the cross provides for them. Temptations will always come. Do not mistake temptation for sin. Being tempted to return to your old sin habits is normal. It is what you do with those temptations that makes all the difference in living free.

Remember you are only human and a strong sin nature is natural for humans. But Jesus, who fights your battles for you, *is supernatural.* And He is the real superhero in this scenario. He is the One who will, by His grace, help you to overcome any issue and temptation you struggle with. It is not up to you to be strong or perfect—just submitted. Again, the latter half of Philippians 3:3 says, "We rely on what Christ Jesus has done for us. We put no confidence in human effort" (NLT). This Scripture holds true for every situation in life, especially when dealing with old sin routines.

When temptation comes, it is the work of the cross, not your strength, you must rely on. I do not know about you, but I love this Scripture! Philippians 3:3 causes me to breathe a sigh of relief.

But maybe relying on Jesus in the middle of fighting temptation seems too difficult for you and you are wondering *how* to rely on Him. The how is simple, not always easy, but simple.

You rely on the work of the cross by submitting to it. When you are struggling with giving into temptation, it is a perfect time to practice the James 4:6–8 method of submission: humble yourself, submit the struggle to God, resist the devil by telling him to flee, draw near to God and He will draw near to you. Then set your heart to live in this drawn-near position. You might have to do this many times, but do not give up. When in a struggle, you need to persist in pressing into Jesus.

Another method you can use that effectively works for me was introduced by my friend, Cathy. She suggested that when I am struggling or if God reveals an empty place in my heart or life to simply invite Jesus into it. Yes, it is that easy. Invite Jesus into the place in your heart, will, emotions, and mind that you are struggling with. I practice this procedure as often as needed. I ask Him to change my heart in my area of weakness. It does not have to be complicated, just a quick recognition and simple prayer. I also like to speak truth (quoting the Word of God) to my area of struggle.

If you struggle with, let us say, pornography (common in our culture), you would first recognize your sin and then invite Jesus into that place of struggle, asking Him to meet you right there in the ugliest place of your heart. He is a friend of sinners, not a condemner, and no sin is too hideous for Him. Next, take a minute to recognize His presence. Let His love for you saturate this dark place; let His love bring you peace and freedom. Now pray God's Word into your situation. In this case it could be Galatians 5:24: "Those who belong to Christ Jesus have nailed the passions and desires of their sinful nature to his cross and crucified them there" (NLT). By faith own the truth of the Scripture; determine to believe that its truth is your truth. When you are in a battle, practice these methods as often as needed.

NOURISH YOUR HEART AND SOUL

The best way I have found to contend for freedom and to continually live in close relationship with Jesus is to nourish my heart and soul with His word. This is how we contend and fill up. To quote Brother Lawrence, "We should feed and nourish our souls with high notions of God which would yield us great joy in being devoted to Him." Our hearts and souls need to be nourished by the things of God.

Feeding the heart and soul is equal to feeding the body. If we consistently fill up with junk food, our bodies will become unhealthy, sick, and weak, which is a reflection of what goes in. A malnourished heart and soul will be immature and will separate from God, becoming rebellious, independent, stubborn, and self-indulgent.

In our house, we have what we call "Bible time." Bible time is basically time set aside to worship, read the Bible, and pray. Please be encouraged to set time aside daily to have your own kind of Bible time. It does not have to be a long, drawn-out religious event. The length of time can vary according to your schedule. Some days more time can be devoted to this, and on busier days, a short psalm or proverb may be all that time will allow. There are many Bible apps available for mobile devices with audio versions of the Bible for home or when you are on the go. The point is to consistently get the Word in you.

A good place to start reading would be one of the first four books of the New Testament. Beginning there will detail the life and personality of Jesus, helping you to get to know Him. If this sounds too overwhelming, maybe you could read a devotional book. Devotionals usually give you small pieces of Scripture, an encouraging word, and a prayer.

A CONTINUOUS WORK

We cannot be passive about living free. Healing is something we can continually partake of because God usually shows us things in stages. New heartaches occur and we always have to deal with our Me-factor issues, new offenses, hurts, misunderstandings, and outright sin. Therefore, we need God to constantly meet us in those places.

When any form of the Me factor rises up, such as pride, a jealous thought, or looking for approval from people, quickly repent, submit, and then invite Jesus into that place. Ask Him to forgive you and fill the depths of your heart.

This practice is a staple for me. As soon as I recognize I have depended on people or things to fill me—this is what I do. And it becomes evident that Jesus is healing my very core where the emptiness stems from. I use the word *emptiness* because any space in our hearts and souls that Jesus does not occupy is indeed empty. This practice is effective for all areas and should become a staple for you as well—something you can use daily for various situations and struggles, whether it be the Me factor, healing, grief, loss, unforgiveness, separation, offenses, and all forms of heartbreak.

OFFENSES

It is not a matter of *if* an offense will come. Believe me—they will come—quite regularly! Offenses come from others, but the option resides within us to be offended or not. It is our choice. With this in mind, we need to be prepared and know how to deal with new offenses. Sometimes when dealing with an offense, it feels as if you are wrestling a huge, relentless creature, but when you persistently stand against it, practicing the method of inviting Jesus into the place of offense, it does cease.

Keep in mind, one who lives in the Me factor has a hard time *not* being offended. Rather, a person who lives submitted to God's Word can love with the same kind of love mentioned in 1 Corinthians 13:5b: "[Love] keeps no record of being wronged" (NLT). And in Philippians 1:10, "That you may approve the things that are excellent, that you may be sincere and without offense till the day of Christ" (NKJV).

The best way to prepare for an offense is to first get your heart and soul into alignment with Jesus and His Word to live a sub-mitted lifestyle. And second, determine to live your life free of offense. Make a choice now not to let anyone or anything have the power to offend you. Easier said than done? Yes, but not impos-sible. Remember, being offended is a choice.

This is all accomplished by making Jesus enough. When we determine to step into an offense-free life, what other people do and say will not offend us because we are so full of Jesus. He has so filled us that people's words and actions do not penetrate; they just fall to the ground, leaving us unaffected. A lot of the time there is a struggle, but this is where you turn to Jesus, choosing to trust Him with the situation. This is where you decide to make Him enough.

Stepping into healing is a choice, one that will catapult you into continual heart hydration. Please do not let fear, shame, or doubt keep you from making the choice to step into Jesus' provision of freedom from strongholds, unhealthy connections, root causes, and offenses. Choose to remember who you are in Christ, and keep in mind—freedom is a staple for those who follow Christ.

10

HEALING SEXUAL BROKENNESS

Even after we give our hearts and souls to Jesus, we can struggle to walk in the freedom the cross has provided for us. One main reason for this struggle can be sexual brokenness, which is pretty common in our culture and a huge cause of heart dehydration. Sexual brokenness is not shameful, nor is it untouchable. It is certainly not something to stuff away and never heal from. Sexual healing will hydrate your heart and soul because it will remove clutter that keeps you from fully engaging in a deeper relationship with Jesus.

The good news is Jesus is not shocked by sexual brokenness or sexual sin. Past mistakes, failures, and bad choices do not matter to Him. Grace causes Him to look beyond it all into the heart of a person. He knows that sin is just a symptom of brokenness. He extends grace, mercy, and unconditional love. He tenderly holds and heals the heart of the hurting. He beckons the broken to come to Him.

I would like to clarify the way I am using the term brokenness. There are two kinds of brokenness. The one I am referring to here (the bad kind) has to do with being wounded and brokenhearted. The other kind of brokenness (the good kind) is described in Psalm 51:17: "The sacrifice you desire is a broken spirit. You will not reject a broken and repentant heart, O God" (NLT). This brokenness means to have a yielded, submitted heart, soul, and life. This is what we want and what has been encouraged throughout this book.

Keep in mind that not everyone wears the dehydration of sexual brokenness where it can be seen. It gets covered up, and people think or pretend they are just fine. But sexual brokenness surfaces in so many outward forms, such as depression, self-protection, perfectionism, selfishness, workaholism, hardheartedness, isolation, overachievement, issues with food, fear of man, performance-based relationships, anger, perversion, pornography, immorality, low self-esteem, pride, vanity, unforgiveness, fear, shame, control, guilt, jealousy, or unbelief. These can also open the doors for strongholds to attach themselves. The point is sexual brokenness cannot be dismissed because a person does not have apparent sexual problems. Please take what you just read from the previous chapter about healing and combine it with what you learn from this chapter to acquire a complete understanding of sexual healing.

Many people believe that time heals all wounds, but this belief equals an empty promise. Time may lessen the pain of the wound, but only God can heal it. There are many ways He does this. In this chapter, you will get a glimpse of how God healed my sexual brokenness and discover tools to help you and those you care about step into freedom.

THE UNMENTIONABLES

Some people may be getting a little uncomfortable right now because we are discussing the "unmentionables" of life and may want to avoid this subject. Relax. Jesus loves you and He is enough. If this subject messes with your comfort zone, simply choose to trust Him. Bring your heart into submission, and make a choice to step into the freedom He has provided for you. Do not let fear or pride steal from you any longer.

I am that person who has no problem talking about the supposedly unmentionable subjects. Why? Because everyone is valuable and deserves to live in the freedom Jesus paid such a high price for. Therefore, I am not ashamed to tell of the unmentionables in my life and in the life of my husband. (By the way, I do have his permission!)

My story is a bit edgy. My purpose in speaking about such things is not to hurt or uncover those involved, but to give hope that will help hydrate your heart by helping you step into healing. I want people to grasp and understand the truth that if Jesus can change me and my husband—heal and deliver us from our dysfunctional lives—then yes, He can bring freedom to you as well. You can step into a lifestyle where your past no longer dictates your future, a life where you, beyond a shadow of a doubt, know who you are and are content to let Jesus be enough for you.

CHRONICLES

I loved my childhood and I think my mom did a great job, her best, in raising my brother and me. She taught good values, took us to the local Catholic church and worked hard. We were well groomed, dressed, and fed. We lived next to great people who became family, we had a dog, and we had a lot of fun. Summer Mondays were my favorite because it was my mom's day off and we spent it at the beach. There are a lot of holes in the tapestry of my childhood, but basically I was deeply loved.

No doubt the missing piece was the lack of a father in my life. Naturally, when I was a child, I did not have this realization. But I vividly remember an elementary school project where I had to draw a picture of my family's Christmas traditions. I drew a picture of my dad and me hanging Christmas lights on our house. First of all, I only remember spending one Christmas with my dad. We never hung lights and we lived in an apartment. When I really think about the drawing, I recognize that little girl, smiling and laughing but hurt, empty, and disappointed, longing for the love, nurture, and relationship with her father.

My dad was an alcoholic and a gambler, and in living that life, he was very selfish with his love, time, and money. He never lived with my family and visited maybe once a month. He was the kind of dad that continually made promises he never kept.

My fatherlessness led to sexual brokenness because his careless attitude, lack of nurture, and absence created a cavern of emptiness in my heart and life that led to rejection, fear, abandonment, and disappointment, allowing them to set their teeth deep into my heart and soul at a young age. I also experienced sexual abuse as a young child. Combined with my father's absence, I developed many issues with trusting God and people. I later unconsciously tried to fill this emptiness with love and approval from the opposite sex, which led to sexual relationships, which led to abortions, which led to further brokenness.

My mom remarried three times. The first two stepfathers came along when I was a child. They both turned out to be huge disappointments, creating more disillusionment of who fathers were supposed to be and distorting my perception of this very important piece to wholeness. My mom remarried for the third time when I was an adult. This man became more of a father to me and more of a grandfather to my kids than my real dad. I am thankful for him.

I got into a serious relationship where I lost my virginity at age fifteen, a relationship that lasted throughout my high school years. I also started drinking on a regular basis. In my sophomore year, this relationship produced two pregnancies, both pregnancies ending in abortion. The day after the first abortion, my boyfriend and I went to the Catholic church we sometimes attended. The two of us were so torn, regretful, and full of shame that we wanted to pray. Interestingly enough, I cannot remember if I asked God to forgive me.

A large poster hung in the foyer of the church. It pictured a trash bag full of bloody, aborted babies (an encouraging thing to have in a church, right?). My broken, unforgiven heart ached for years at the remembrance of that poster and with the reality of what I had done. My sleep was flooded with strange dreams of blood, abortion, bloody babies, and murder. Shame and condemnation knocked loudly on my conscience. I buried my pain, shame, and regret ever so deeply as I searched for love, wholeness, and relief in all my relationships.

Although this young man and I loved each other, there was a lot of unfaithfulness in our relationship. I never slept around, but my heart did wander. As I look back, I see the attention I got from boys was how I measured my self-worth. It amazes me how much time it took to fully heal from the relationship with my high school sweetheart. I carried on with life, but decades after our breakup, I was still breaking ties and receiving healing. Decades! (Does that astonish anyone but me?)

Even after becoming a Christian, I was still too insecure to be without a boyfriend. I had a couple of "Christian" relationships, which unfortunately included sex. This can be accredited to naïve Christianity. It would have been very helpful if a seasoned, fellow believer would have taught me the ropes. I knew it was wrong to have sex outside of marriage, but I did not know how to walk out biblical principles. I had no idea how damaged I was inside.

Shortly after my high school relationship ended, I met a handsome, very kind guy at church. We briefly dated, then I got pregnant and four months later, married him. Little did I know there was a difference between saying you are a Christian and actually being one.

Both my husband and I were in need of heart hydration. He was the youngest of eight children raised by an alcoholic mother and a detached father. He was sexually abused as well and started having sex and using drugs and alcohol at a very young age. His upbringing lacked nurture and discipline. Are you starting to get the picture? Two broken people get married—a recipe for dysfunction!

When we married, we thought our search for wholeness, security, love, and acceptance would end. We soon discovered not only were we still as empty as ever, but we now had new issues to deal with.

A lot of people make the mistake of expecting their spouse to fill their emptiness and end up feeling very unfulfilled in their marriage. Jesus is the only one who can heal and fill our longing for wholeness.

My husband and I asked Jesus into our hearts but did not make Him our Lord. Our lives were our own. In the following years, we were happy and raised wonderful children together, but our brokenness and insecurities fed off of each other. We did not understand our identity in Christ or the power of the cross, nor did we have a relationship of any depth with Jesus.

My husband's adultery issues started early in our marriage. Although we did not realize it, he suffered from a wounded and unhealed heart and soul. He wanted to love God with his whole heart and be faithful, but he was steeped in brokenness and rejection. He was held tight by strongholds of unbelief, pride, selfishness, rebellion, and independence. His lack of faith and weakness to sin made him think he was worthless. He lived with a lot of shame and guilt, which helped keep him in a continual cycle of sin.

God, in His mercy, uncovered my husband's secret life of continual unfaithfulness, bringing him to repentance. It took decades for my husband's heart and lifestyle to change. But throughout this time, I have had a front row seat to the mercy, grace, and longsuffering of God. He never gave up on my husband (or on me) but continually and ever so tenderly loved him to change.

Four years into our marriage was when our two-year-old daughter Haylie Anne and my only brother died. Already drenched in rejection, disappointment, and abandonment issues, my husband's unfaithfulness and the deaths sent me into a pit of sorrow and despair. One day shortly after my daughter's death, at twenty-five years old and eight months pregnant with my third child, I found myself sitting on the bathroom floor seriously contemplating suicide (the thought of my five-year-old son quickly brought me to my senses).

The reality was my problems were not just from the incidents that took place, but from my unhealed, unresolved brokenness from my past. I was not equipped, meaning I did not have a very solid foundation. I did not know how to make Jesus enough for my heart, soul, and life. My fragile life could not support the new trials I was dealing with.

AND SO IT BEGAN

Fast forward ten years to my midthirties, when I began to step into healing. Up to this point, I stuffed my pain very deeply. A popular saying during this time was "get bitter or get better." My heart was shattered, and I did not know how to get better. And that was precisely my problem. I kept trying to get better, to get over my pain, to ignore it and not deal with the root causes for it. The following allegory describes the condition of my heart and soul. Visualize what I have told you about my life:

Imagine me wearing a huge, oversized, winter cloak. It is a raggedy, dirty, wool garment with many layers. It drapes and drags on the ground as I wear it. Although it is unnecessary, I always wear it—never taking it off even though it causes me to stumble and sink low beneath the weight of it. It is an uncomfortable distraction to have on my shoulders, yet it is familiar and warm.

At times, the pain of wearing the cloak seems unbearable, causing grouchiness and impatience, leading me to lash out at those I love. The smell of this heavy, burdensome cloak is putrid. It makes it difficult to get close to people. After a while, I attempt to cover it up, trying to disguise it by spraying expensive perfume on it so no one will notice. It is stressful to maintain this heaviness, but removing it would be way too exhausting. I have worn it for so long that it is embedded in my skin. It would be too embarrassing to uncover myself at this point and far too painful to get free now.

What is interesting is that for most of my life, I did not even know I was wearing it. I carried around my brokenness, wearing my sexual wounds as a cloak. I believe I put it on in childhood to mask my pain from my father's rejection and from sexual abuse. Layers of this cloak were added with each new incident. Wearing this cover-up of self-protection helped me deal with my life. The cloak hid who I really was, making me, among many things, very insecure, striving for people's approval.

Through the healing power of the cross and Jesus' faithful love, I began to step into healing and remove the cloak. Layer after layer, He gently removed it, healing me. The bottom line of my sexual brokenness was mistrust. As Jesus removed each layer, I exchanged the pain and mistrust for healing and faithful love, and over time He taught me how to trust Him, showing me He was not at all like the people who had hurt and betrayed me.

As I continued in the process of removing the cloak, I found myself blaming God for Haylie's death and my pain. Although I did not want to admit it, I was angry at Him for her death—angry because I felt He had let me down—angry because, to say the least, I figured He had disappointed me.

Healing from this began one morning when I vividly pictured myself shaking my fist at God. As I repented, He spoke to my heart saying, "Why don't you shake your fist at the evil one where it will do you some good?" That encounter brought so much clarity and healing because it helped me see who my real enemy was. As I shifted my anger, my perspective changed and I was able to see the devil's part in the whole thing: to steal, kill, and destroy my faith, family, marriage, and destiny. He, without hesitation, took advantage of my brokenheartedness and tried to get me to turn my back on Jesus. The devil, the enemy of our soul, is the author of the blame-shifting game and unsuccessfully tried to manipulate my heart and soul to blame God.

My perspective change helped me to refocus. I was able to stop blaming God for Haylie's death and invite His love into the depths of my heart. In my marriage, I began to see how my husband was not my enemy. Concerning sexual abuse and my father issues, I could see how the enemy of my soul always had a plan to destroy my life.

Receiving healing from the sexual abuse was unexpected. It was unexpected because I had buried the memories so deeply that I never thought about it. Little did I know receiving healing from this would set me free to trust and love in ways I had not experienced. The Lord revealed the incidents, asked me to forgive the perpetrators, and then filled me with His healing love. It was not a long process. It was painful but not devastating—mainly because

153

I was able to invite Jesus into the hurt places in my heart. As I let Him into the unmentionable places, He healed me, comforted me, and removed my shame.

As my healing continued, I constantly had this vision of myself: I was driving down the freeway and my car broke down. There I was stranded on the side of the road and God the Father drove by and just looked at me and did not stop to help—just left me there on the side of the road, helpless, to fend for myself. Through that visualization, I was able to recognize that in my heart, that was how I saw my father and how I saw God—capable of loving and helping me but never willing to take the time.

At this point, God whispered to my heart, "I am not at all like your biological father." For years, every time I doubted Him or equated Him to my dad, He would say these words to me. Each time He spoke them, the truth of His love penetrated my heart and soul a little deeper, healing me and resetting my core belief about God—my loving Father.

I broke unhealthy connections with my biological father and broke the strongholds off my heart and soul that came from his rejection, abandonment, and disappointment. Healing from my father's rejection was a long process because, as stated earlier, I equated God the Father with my biological father. Consequently, it was difficult to trust Him with my heart for fear He would treat me as my father did.

When people are rejected by their parents, it changes their sense of self-worth and causes them to lose the truth about who they are in Christ. For me, my father's actions caused me to think I was not valuable, caused me to look for love and acceptance from the opposite sex, which led to giving my heart and body away. The healing process, amongst many things, included discarding the lie that I was worthless, which helped me to step into the truth of who I am.

Healing from my husband's sin against me was laced throughout the years. I broke unhealthy ties and strongholds concerning him many times. A huge portion happened when Jesus asked me to make Him enough and for me to be a bridge to my husband. I was a bit angry at what He was asking. My response was, *Really God? Lay down my life to be walked on by the person who has hurt me the most? What about my rights as a human being?*

Jesus' response was, "Let Me sustain you."

Being a bridge to my husband was about him finding Jesus as his Savior. At this point, Jesus told me there was nothing more important than a person's salvation—not even my freedom from the pain of my marriage. My husband was so damaged from his life that he did not trust many people. But he did trust me. I was the one who could make him or break him. I was the one person who mattered to him and who could show him unconditional love that would help him understand the love of God.

I, with a clean heart, could not say no to what Jesus was asking of me. In fact, on our thirtieth anniversary, by the grace of God, I said, "Lord I'm willing to do this for thirty more years if that is what it takes. Nothing is worth him going to hell." Thirty years was just thirty years, but hell—that would be for eternity.

This is when my heart received the majority of healing from my husband's unfaithfulness. It was when I realized I had nothing in me to do what Jesus was asking, and I had to press into Jesus more than I ever had before. I had to let Him be enough—let Him sustain me.

Psalm 55:22 says, "Cast your burden on the LORD, and He shall sustain you; He shall never permit the righteous to be moved" (NKJV). I clung to this Scripture! Sustain means to bear the weight of, to endure without yielding, and to keep from giving way under any affliction, trial, or pressure. Ponder this and imagine Jesus as your Sustainer. This is an amazing promise—oh, the goodness of God!

Every time (probably a million times a day) when I felt I could not love this man in the capacity Jesus was asking of me, I would think of Jesus as my Sustainer. I would picture myself as an actual bridge: laid out, stretched beyond my own capacity and comfort zone, and underneath me was Jesus, my support, bearing me up, believing in me, and encouraging me to do the impossible. The healing came as I trusted Jesus to be enough for me and turned my heart to live my life under His shadow, in His presence, close to His heart (Psalm 91:1–4).

THE HEALING PROCESS

Healing usually starts when we recognize our brokenness. Faithful God will reveal past experiences, memories, or hidden pockets of emptiness, pain, wounds, strongholds, or ties residing in our hearts and souls. When the process begins, it is not uncommon to feel as if our life is unraveling. What is really important to keep in mind is that it is just a season. It will not last forever; therefore, we must resolve to stay with it.

After the recognition stage comes the forgiveness stage. Yes, the "f" word again. Forgiveness is essential to any healing process, especially sexual healing—even if you have been sinned against. You must forgive, even if the people who sinned against you never confess, repent, or apologize.

Also, no matter what you have been through, you must forgive and ask for forgiveness for your sin in the matter. *My sin in the matter?* Yes. We are always responsible for our response. If we sin in our reaction to sin committed against us, then yes, we are responsible for our sin. Just because someone sins against us, we are not given a free pass to hold hate, anger, offense, or bitterness in our hearts against them. Jesus is our example.

My first encounter with forgiveness was with the abortions. When I first became a Christian, I asked God to forgive me, and I had to first receive His forgiveness then extend it to others. I had to forgive myself, my boyfriend, and other people who pushed me to have the abortions. Jesus' forgiveness in this matter brought freedom from the shame and guilt that I had dealt with. I also had relief from the bad dreams I used to have about my abortions.

My next major appointment with forgiveness was the first time I had to forgive my husband for unfaithfulness. I will never forget how surprised I was when our pastor said I had to forgive him. My husband had sinned against me, and she was informing me I had to forgive him. My jaw literally dropped. *What? Let him off?* She went on to explain something about growing bitter if I did not and so on and so on…her words numbed my thoughts. That was my first realization of what forgiving others was really all about. From that point on, I have had many opportunities to forgive my husband and others. In the middle of one of those times, Matthew 18:21–22 became my truth.

Then Peter came to Him and said, "Lord, how often shall my brother sin against me, and I forgive him? Up to seven times?" Jesus said to him, "I do not say to you, up to seven times, but up to seventy times seven." (NKJV)

Verses 23–33 go on to tell a story that is all too familiar to our human condition. We find it so easy to receive forgiveness, and we gladly invite Jesus to wipe away our debts. But unfortunately in our next breath, we can turn to those whom we need to forgive and relentlessly demand repayment for the wrongs they have committed against us, all the while forgetting what was done for us.

Through this passage, I could plainly see I was the one who owed more than I could repay. I had committed murder not once but twice when I aborted my babies. I could never repay that debt. Thank Jesus He paid it for me on the cross. What unconditional love and forgiveness! The Master canceled my debt, and I was practically wringing my husband's neck (with my unforgiveness, revenge, and hate), demanding repayment for his sin against me.

Another very important part about forgiveness is the freedom it brings to our mind and emotions. Matthew 18:34 says the ungrateful servant was turned over to the torturers. As I held on to unforgiveness, I was tormented in my thoughts night and day. Satan's access to my mind was the open door of unforgiveness that I was struggling to shut. My own thoughts were my worst enemy. Forgiveness unquestionably is hydrating.

SEX TIES YOU TO ANOTHER PERSON

The next step in the sexual healing/hydration process is disconnecting your heart and soul from people you have connected with sexually (not just intercourse but all forms of sexual behavior). Again, it is good to do this because sex ties two people together. Ephesians 5:31b says, "The two shall become one flesh" (NKJV). Sex attaches two people and they become one; it links their hearts and souls together. Sex in marriage is part of the adhesive God uses to keep couples together. Severing unhealthy connections over your heart and soul may be a foreign concept to you, but why would you want to go through life with your heart and soul knit to anyone except your spouse? This is especially true if you were sexually abused or raped. Ponder this.

If you need to sever unhealthy sexual connections, first make a list of all the people you need to disconnect yourself from (you can burn it afterwards!). Sometimes this can be very hard or discouraging to do. Understandable. This is a perfect place to make

Jesus enough and to ask Him to pour His love and grace in you—to strengthen you.

If there are a lot of people to list, or if the people on the list bring back bad memories, it is okay. Keep in mind you are doing this to get free from these people and from their influence in your life. Be happy they are on this list—because it means you will no longer be subject to them or to the memories associated with them. This is your time to step into your freedom! Please do not shy away from it. The prayer to sever unhealthy sexual connections is at the end of this chapter.

SEX IS MORE THAN SKIN TO SKIN

Sexual sin affects our whole person: body, soul, heart, and spirit and our past, present, and future. First Corinthians 6:16–20 from *The Message* bluntly states,

There's more to sex than mere skin on skin. [1] Sex is as much spiritual mystery as physical fact. As written in Scripture, "The two become one." [2] Since we want to become spiritually one with the Master, we must not pursue the kind of sex that [3] avoids commitment and intimacy, [4] leaving us more lonely than ever—[5] the kind of sex that can never "become one." [6] There is a sense in which sexual sins are different from all others. [7] In sexual sin we violate the sacredness of our own bodies, these bodies that were made for God-given and God-modeled love, for "becoming one" with another. [8] Or didn't you realize that your body is a sacred place, the place of the Holy Spirit? Don't you see that you can't live however you please, [9] squandering what God paid such a high price for? The physical part of you is not some piece of property belonging to the spiritual part of you.

God owns the whole works. So let people see God in and through your body.

I love *The Message* version of these verses. Following are nine points from 1 Corinthians 6:16–20 detailing how sexual sin affects the whole person:

1. Knits two souls together
2. Hinders intimate relationship with Jesus
3. Avoids commitment and intimacy
4. Leaves people lonelier and emptier than before they had sex
5. Can never produce a sacred and blessed intimate bond between two people
6. Is more dangerous than any other sin
7. Affects the body more than any other kind of sin
8. Defiles the temple of the Holy Spirit
9. Dishonors and disregards Jesus' sacrifice on the cross

Sexual sins cause sexual woundedness. Sexual wounds cover a very wide range: from child molestation to rape, teenage promiscuity to immorality, premarital sex to dysfunctional marriage, adultery to one-night stands, prostitution to homosexuality, masturbation to fantasies and pornography, same-sex attraction to gender confusion—just to mention a few. Sexual brokenness shapes and defines people, but for believers in Christ, this should not be the case. The cross, the blood, the empty grave bought our freedom and should be what shapes and defines us. Severing unhealthy connections is just a tool we can use to step into this freedom.

The final and probably the most important step in this healing process after severing unhealthy sexual connections is to exchange your pain and invite Jesus to heal you. Remember, the cross is a place of exchange. Bring your wounds, brokenness, and sin to Jesus and leave them at the cross. Now invite Jesus into the place you relinquished and take back the opposite of what you just left at the cross (forgiveness and freedom). This is where your emptiness is filled and your brokenness made whole.

FEAR IS A BULLY

Even with all the information available about healing and freedom, some people still live with a dehydrated heart and soul, holding tight to their cloak of sexual brokenness. Some choose to hold on to it because in their brokenness, it is all they know. Others suffer from identity issues and do not even know they are wearing one and think this is just who they are. And yet other people are incapacitated by fear, refusing to even start the process of removing the cloak. Fear is a huge bully that keeps people in bondage. Please do not let it keep you from moving forward in your healing process.

When my husband was in the thick of his brokenness, I asked him why he did not choose to step into freedom. His answers were as follows:

- Fear of the unknown: I know how to live like this, and I am afraid to live differently.
- Fear of facing who I really am: I am afraid of the kind of person I have become.
- Fear of facing the root cause: The past is a painful place to visit.
- Fear of not being accepted: Once people know who I really am, they will reject me.
- Fear of pain: I have ignored the pain of my childhood for so long, so why face it now?
- Fear of pain to others: I have caused enough pain to those I love already.
- Fear of the freedom process: Getting free is painful, time consuming, and embarrassing.

- Fear of the cost to become free: What will be lost in the process?
- Denial: If I ignore it, it will go away.

Fear is a façade and only has the power you give it. Fear bullies people into thinking their only choice is to stay in their current prison of brokenness, sin, and shame—just the opposite of grace and truth. Second Timothy 1:7 clearly states, "For God has not given us a spirit of fear, but of power and of love and of a sound mind" (NKJV). This is the believer's reality. This is who we are.

I understood my husband's fear, but what I came to understand even clearer was that he was broken. His greatest need was to surrender His heart and soul to Jesus and let Him heal his sexual brokenness. He needed healing from all that had transpired in his past and from his sin choices. He was hurting, and the sexual sin was just a symptom of much deeper issues.

If you can identify fear as a bully in your life, I urge you to take the steps mentioned in the previous chapter to deal with it. Also, please realize the freedom you already have as a believer in Jesus and His accomplished work on the cross.

PRAYER TO SEVER UNHEALTHY SEXUAL CONNECTIONS

Before severing unhealthy sexual connections, finish this chapter and then refer to the previous chapter, "Healing the Heart and Soul." Go through the root-cause procedure and pray to break any strongholds that you may be stuck in. Also sever all unhealthy connections that are not sexual.

The next step is to sever unhealthy sexual connections, and I have included a prayer to help as you take this step. Of course, you can tailor it to fit your individual situation. My prayer is long but thorough. Personally, I did not want to leave anything undone.

You can pray alone or with a pastor, family member, or friend who understands this manner of prayer. It is very important to remember after severing each connection to invite Jesus into the place where the tie has been severed, asking Him to heal and fill you. Relax—God loves you and only has good plans for you!

Jesus, please forgive me for my inappropriate behavior with _____. Forgive me for linking my heart, soul, body, and affections with _____. I truly am sorry for the damage I have caused my own heart, soul, body, and spirit. I see that my sin was not only against You but against my whole person and my future. Thank you that the power of the cross has healed and delivered me from the root causes of my sin. Today I step into this truth. I renounce and sever every connection with _____. I sever it over my heart, mind, will, emotions, body, spirit, my past, and my future. I forgive _____ and all involved. I forgive myself. Forgive me for finding my self-worth, identity, and value from this person's view and acceptance of me. I disconnect myself from the person I was at that time and from the tie of who I used to be. I am no longer that weak, immature, hurt, fragmented, grasping person. I am free, forgiven, pure, and maturing daily. Strengthen me and my faith to stand firm in your grace and in the truth of who I am. Thank you, Jesus! Amen.

STEP INTO HIS HEALING LOVE

Okay, let's summarize what you have learned about this healing process:

- Recognize Jesus as your Healer and Deliverer.
- Recognize that the cross has already bought your freedom.
- Choose to step into your freedom.

- Set your heart to fall in love with Jesus.
- Know the Holy Spirit.
- Recognize your brokenness.
- Confess and repent.
- Forgive.
- Recognize and deal with strongholds.
- Recognize and deal with root causes.
- Deal with fear—do not let it bully you.
- Sever all unhealthy connections.
- Know how to stay free.

If any of this is unclear, please reread the section you need clarity on so that you may gain a greater understanding of this healing process.

What are you thinking right now? Is Jesus in His faithfulness tugging at your heart? Is He gently pressing tender, forgotten areas of your past, wanting to heal you? Maybe your wounds are not sexual, but you still may need healing. Please do not shrug God off. Take this opportunity to seek Jesus and ask Him to reveal areas of brokenness, sexual or otherwise, in your heart and soul. Jesus has so generously provided healing hydration and freedom for you—step into it!

11
YOU'VE GOT THIS

I have a love-hate relationship with reading books. I love to read them, but I hate when I get to the end. Books have a way of becoming a part of who I am, and I am always a little sad to end my reading journey. And although I do not know you personally, I feel as if I have been personally writing to you and sharing the deepest part of my life with you. Therefore, even though I am not the reader, I still am a bit sad to come to the end.

I hope and pray that you will embrace all that has been communicated with you about heart hydration. Maybe you are ready to dive headfirst into all the methods I have mentioned. Or maybe you are saying, "Oh, hell no. This is not for me!" I would be lying if I said that was not my first reaction! But as you know, all the work involved is well worth the effort.

Whether you are the person who is fully embracing heart hydration or if you are the one who is hesitant, please remember you are in a process, as we all are, and you don't ever have to be perfect; just set your heart to make progress. Be encouraged to step into a deeper personal relationship with Jesus. This relationship, which I am sure you understand by now, is the very essence of heart hydration.

Believing and knowing the truth of who you are in Christ is actually the most important step of all. Please take the needed time to really let the facts of who you are in Him to sink in deeply. I don't say this only because it is a good thing to say, but because I know, with my whole heart, how valuable you are. You have such great potential and purpose. Do not settle for average!

Let the truth of this cause you to step into the extravagant provision of the cross. This provision is yours. If you were not so important to God, He never would have sent His Son as a ransom for you. You do not have to pitch a tent on the lawn of all Jesus has for you. Never be content to just admire His Word—you are better than that. That kind of lifestyle is not good enough for you. Please be encouraged to step into all Jesus has for you!

I am confident from all you have read about hydrating a thirsty heart that you are hopeful. If there was light at the end of my dark tunnel, then you can be sure there is light at the end of your tunnel. Freedom from the past, from fear, from the Me factor, and from brokenness is completely attainable. The steps to quench a thirsty heart are not unreasonable. Jesus' perfect unconditional love bridged the gap between living a performance-based life of rules to living in the freedom of a grace-based relationship.

Does submission still sound too much like a bad word to you? If so, you know what to do. And that is seeking a change of heart regarding the Me factor and living in submission. I promise you as your heart changes, you will be able to step into the freedom of relationship that is not all bound up in powerless religion (2 Timothy 3:5). Instead, grace will make a way for you.

Embracing submission catapults you into the reality that Jesus is enough for you *personally.* Remember, you do not have to be perfect—just submitted. Living this lifestyle removes the heavy burden of striving to be good enough for God and others. This truth eliminates jostling for position and the worry and stress of living a performance-based life. Not only will striving cease, but your heart will be full and satisfied. Psalm 23 will be your reality. As you read it, savor every word. Take it in, and as you do, realize this is your portion in life.

The LORD is my shepherd; I shall not want. He makes me to lie down in green pastures; He leads me beside the still waters. He restores my soul; He leads me in the paths of righteousness for His name's sake. Yea, though I walk through the valley of the shadow of death, I will fear no evil; for You are with me; Your rod and Your staff, they comfort me. You prepare a table before me in the presence of my enemies; You anoint my head with oil; my cup runs over. Surely goodness and mercy shall follow me all the days of my life; and I will dwell in the house of the LORD forever. (NKJV)

No want, no lack, no need because Jesus is enough—such an amazing promise! This sounds inviting, right? He becomes enough when you step into complete trust in His faithfulness.

Go ahead, jump.

Leap off the mountain of doubt and unbelief; dive heart-first into the truth of God's love, grace, and trustworthiness.

Leave worry, apprehension, and fear behind. Strengthen your faith to believe as the heroes of faith in Hebrews 11 believed. I love what verse 4 says about faith: "By an act of faith, Abel brought a better sacrifice to God than Cain. It was what he *believed*, not what he *brought*, that made the difference. That's what God noticed and approved as righteous. After all these centuries, that belief continues to catch our notice" (Hebrews 11:4, MSG). This Scripture makes things so clear. It was what Abel "*believed*, not what he *brought*" that caught God's attention. If moving forward in heart hydration seems too difficult, or maybe you think you need to get your life and heart together before you step into it, please take time to understand this Scripture. It is NOT what you bring to God that matters; it is your faith that matters.

Please let your faith out of the box of impossibilities and into the actuality of Mark 9:23b: "Everything is possible for one who believes" (NIV). Dare to expect Jesus to be faithful. Live in the truth that it is against His character to be unfaithful. Make this your motto about Jesus.

Change your perspective about Him and begin to live with a heart-style of thanksgiving. Quench your thirst with thankfulness. Take a big drink and taste how being thankful takes you from a complaining heart to a grateful, satisfied attitude of praise.

Filling your heart with appreciation causes your heart and soul to be so hydrated that you have no problem honoring God with obedience, because now you understand what it means to revere and live in awe of God. You understand that obeying God equals loving God. And you know that if He did not love you so radically, so jealously, He would not ask you to live in obedience.

THE THRIVING HEART AND SOUL

I encourage you to live in the importance of nourishing your heart and soul with the Word. Step into a lifestyle of praying without ceasing. Continually converse with Jesus and watch your heart and soul thrive.

Your heart must be soaring at all the new possibilities of freedom. Words like deliverance, stronghold, healing, and sexual broken- ness no longer cause you to be fearful. You are not afraid because the perfect love of Jesus defeated fear and you are free to take Jesus at His Word (1 John 4:18).

You completely understand now that Jesus does not put shame, excessive guilt, and condemnation on you—that is the devil's job. Jesus loves you, sees past your weakness, and heals your broken heart. Sexual brokenness has lost its grip. Walking in forgiveness is your new reality. You can confidently step out of your comfort zone and step into healing and wholeness—they are not out of your reach. You no longer have to lug around your old cloak of brokenness.

Most of all, you are not afraid of the healing process; stepping into freedom does not intimidate you. Your heart and soul are aching for hydration, eager to live in closer relationship with Jesus—in the very heart of God—and experience His audacious love.

Lastly, I encourage and challenge you to accept the invitation given in Isaiah 55:1–3:

> Hey there! All who are thirsty, come to the water! Are you penniless? Come anyway—buy and eat! Come, buy your drinks, buy wine and milk. Buy without money—everything's free! Why do you spend your money on junk food, your hard-earned cash on cotton candy? Listen to me, listen well: Eat only the best, fill yourself with only the finest. Pay attention, come close now, listen carefully to my life-giving, life-nourishing words. I'm making a lasting covenant commitment with you, the same that I made with David: sure, solid, enduring love. (MSG)

Are you thirsty for heart hydration? Are you ready to step into the grace of God? Are you ready to step into every provision the cross bought for you?

Go ahead—you've got this!

Do not delay. He is waiting.

NOTES

NOTES

NOTES

ACKNOWLEDGMENTS

I am so thankful for the faithfulness of Jesus. His love so deep, His grace so wide, and His promises so true. The divine Beachcomber picked up all the broken pieces of my life, heart, and marriage and put them together more beautiful than ever before.

Thank you, John, for always believing in me as a person and as a writer. Thank you for loving me. Especially, thank you for never giving up and for allowing our story to be told. I am grateful for your grit, tireless work ethic, and provision for our rather large family—allowing me to stay home. Thanks for making life so fun and spontaneous—I am so happy to grow old with you. I love you! You are my favorite human!

Thank you to my dear sweet children—Joshua, Charles, Faith, Maddison, Parker, and Silas. Each of you warms and fills my heart. You make life worth living. It is a pleasure, blessing, and so much fun to be your mom! Thank you for your care and tenderness toward me. Thank you for your forgiveness and understanding. Also, thank you for believing in me and this book—for enduring with me all the countless hours on the computer, and for all the ways you have been there for me during this long process. I love you. I am proud of you, and I believe in you. You are my favorites!

Bryson, Sage, and Robbie Girl, you are so dear to my heart. You are my sunshine. I love you!

Kaila, Trent, Micheal, Breann, Laura, and Candis, I am so thankful that you are part of this crazy family! Thank you for your support. I love and cherish you.

Charles, thank you for being my go-to guy and for all your wisdom with websites, video, contracts, and business.

Trent and Jason, thank you for your priceless creativity in designing the cover.

Maddison, thank you for the foreword. You are a woman of the deepest beauty, filled with His wisdom.

Mom, thank you for taking me to St. Benedict's that treasured night we gave our hearts to Jesus. You always did a great job—your best—in raising us kids. I appreciate your hard work and sacrifices. Also, thanks for giving birth to me on your birthday and for always sharing what was supposed to be your special day with me! I love you so much.

Pop, thank you for all you do. I love you.

I would like to especially acknowledge Wilma Dee Benson, who truly lived her life for an audience of One. She was my spiritual mom, mentor, and friend. I will forever be grateful for her love, support, and wisdom. My life and the lives of my family were made rich through my relationship with her. She is loved and missed by many.

A special thank you to my two best friends, Cathy Brookshire and Teresa Elling. Thank you for decades of friendship and enduring love. You are my sisters, voices of wisdom, confidantes, and heroes! Your graciousness never ceases to amaze me. You girls have patiently stood by me, believed in me, cried with me, cried for me, taught me, encouraged me, prayed for me, and most of all, you have faithfully pointed me to Jesus. God is so faithful to give me friends like you. I appreciate you. Thank you for your constant prayers for the book and for all your input and help with it. I love you and your amazing families!

Cathy, your friendship helped sustain me in the darkest of days. Most of the concepts in this book have come from your wisdom. Thank you!

Thank you to my dear friends Sheryl Bishop, Shannon Foust, Danett Arroyo, and Debbie Harman for your invaluable friendship, love, prayers, and support. I love you and your families! I am so thankful for you.

Thank you to my editors: Kim Foster, Danett Arroyo, Kathy Davidson, Teresa Elling, and Kevin Rensink. Oh my gosh, what can I say? There is a special place in heaven for editors—especially my editors! You are the real heroes in the completion of this book! Thank you for taking time out of your busy lives to work on this project. I am forever grateful! I love you!

Thank you to my sweet friend Dr. Beth Earnest, for encouraging and challenging me to expand my faith and knowledge of the Word. Also, thank you for your prayers and for tirelessly ministering to the needs of those around you. I love and appreciate you.

Pastor Steve and Taunia Meistrell, thank you for your wisdom, influence, and prayer support. Most importantly, thank you for raising such an amazing son!

Cindy Anderson, thank you for your encouragement all those years back to write. Also, for teaching me that writing a book is equal to building the Great Wall of China—one section (chapter) at a time.

Thank you to the many people who have met with me over the years and let God, through *Thirsty Heart*, change your lives—

you know who you are. I appreciate your tenacity! I love and believe in you!

I would also like to acknowledge Kathleen Lopez—because of her prayers and kindness, I was introduced to Jesus.

Thank you, Carl Tuttle, for being such a gracious, caring, and fun pastor. John and I are forever grateful for your love and support in our darkest times—especially when Haylie died and that unforgettable night in 1989 when heaven touched earth. The way you loved and pastored us changed our lives. We love you and appreciate you. And by the way, we will never be able to look at another Hostess raspberry-filled donut and not think of you!

Many thanks to all the people who have prayed for me and for *Thirsty Heart*.

Before I was even born, Catherine Marshall wrote a book titled *Beyond Our Selves*. And later a woman named Nancy Guthrie wrote *Holding On to Hope*. These books encouraged and challenged me in countless ways. When my life fell apart, God used the truth held in these two books to help heal and change my heart. I thank and acknowledge these women for telling their stories, which inspired me to write mine.

THIRSTY HEART STUDY GUIDE

NOURISHMENT FOR A DEHYDRATED SOUL

Drink even deeper.
Refresh your soul
with the easy-to-use
THIRSTY HEART
Study Guide.

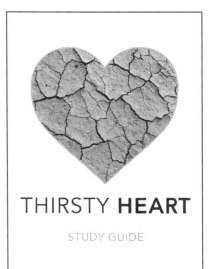

THIRSTY **HEART**

STUDY GUIDE

REGINA FOREST

THIRSTY **HEART**

52 WEEK
DEVOTIONAL

REGINA FOREST

THIRST-QUENCHING SIPS FOR A THIRSTY HEART

52-WEEK DEVOTIONAL

The layout is simple,
quick, and easy to use.

Quick Sips
52 weeks a year—5 days a
week—5 minutes a day of
thirst-quenching sips.

Coming Soon!

28903831R00098

Made in the USA
Columbia, SC
26 October 2018